WHITE STAR

CONTENTS

INTRODUCTION	PAGE 8
THE MISTS OF TIME	PAGE 18
ARMOR: THE INHERITANCE OF THE SEA	PAGE 40
ARGOAT: THE 'LAND OF WOODS'	PAGE 98
THE AWAKENING OF IDENTITY	PAGE 126
INDEX	PAGE 134

© 2004 White Star S.r.l.
Via Candido Sassone, 22/24
13100 Vercelli, Italy
www.whitestar.it

TRANSLATION
STUDIO VECCHIA, MILAN

All rights reserved. This book, or any portion thereof, may not be reproduced in any form without written permission of the publisher.

ISBN 88-540-0018-3

REPRINTS:
1 2 3 4 5 6   08 07 06 05 04
Printed in China by Leefung
Color separation: Chiaroscuro, Turin

Brittany

PLACES AND HISTORY

Text by Thierry Jigourel

10 top Pays Bigouden, a region in the south of Brittany, extends from the right bank of the Odet River to the Bay of Audierne. The coastline offers splendid beaches and, in places, extremely evocative rocky stretches.

10-11 The Créac'h lighthouse, one of the many that dot the Île d'Ouessant, a rocky promontory on the ocean, an indication of the entrance to the English Channel.

11 Given Brittany's rocky, tide-swept shores, lighthouses are a particularly recurrent architectural theme.

14-15 Giving onto the Place du Champ Jacquet, these buildings in the city of Rennes are splendid examples of rush-mat houses.

16-17 On festive occasions, even the youngest turn out in charming costumes, creating a very joyful picture despite the solemnity of the celebrations.

Bretón poet Saint-Pol-Roux. This "balcony on the sea" is a mixture of diverse landscapes.

"Brittany: woods within, sea without," echoed the sweet poet Brizeau in the 19th century, charmed by the ruins and the delightful dizziness of their origins. These worlds, by themselves, summarize the profound, perennial and fundamental dualism of a land divided in men's eyes into two entirely different entities with a climate that is milder on the coast and harsher and less sunny inland, with human activity, the fishing of Armor and the agriculture of Argoat and, above all, with the vegetation. Was this not already succinctly expressed in 1533 by Charles Estienne in his *Guide des chemins de France*. " ... The duchy of Brittany, from ancient times called Armorica, is shaped like a horseshoe, the edges of which are more or less the sea and, for this reason, are called in the vernacular Armoros, which is to say "land of the sea." The bottom or hollow of this figure is on *terra firma* with moors and its common name is *ar goet* ..."

Brittany, in the end, is a legacy from which comes the need — or rather the imperative — for the transmission of an important, even essential part of the identity of our continent.

And though it is true that the Breton conscience is still little known in the great political movements that agitate other nations without countries, the people of the region, freed now of their old complexes and proud of their re-found voice, of their rich music and their roots, finally dare to look into the future with serenity.

And this is the Brittany, always a little rebellious, as Victor Hugo said, which dares and thinks, the Brittany that we wanted you to see. Or rather, glimpse, since describing an entire country in few pages is a very large challenge.

The *Tro Breizh*, the tour of Brittany, to which we invite you, is the result of a choice, naturally a subjective one. It is the result of the enthusiasm of the author who wished to emphasize certain aspects,

the most authentic ones, rather than describing everything systematically, ending by offering a collection of postcard stereotypes. What this work loses in completeness, it undoubtedly gains in sincerity. May this excursion into the "holy ground" of Brittany, to paraphrase Gwenc'hlan Le Scouézec, give you the desire to continue your voyage which, like all voyages in the Celtic world, can be nothing more than an initiation. This book has no other aim. *Digemer mat e Breizh!*

THE MISTS OF TIME

18 top This series of ceramic forms from the 3rd millenium B.C., displayed in the Museum of St.-Germain-en-Laye, come from the site of Conguel, at the tip of the Quiberon peninsula.

18 bottom Archeological finds from the end of the Eneolithic era include bronze and gold objects, for example, this splendid half-moon discovered in Saint-Potan.

Haven't many historians, even the most eminent ones, perhaps begun the history of Brittany with the arrival or even the settlement of the Celts? This is no doubt due to the fact that its pre-historic era is still immersed in a fog so dense that even the mists of Avalon vanish in comparison. In this way, however, our most remote ancestors are reduced to a mere walk-on role! They become shadows with no other name than a "pre" or a "proto" with which we render unconvincing homage to figures that vanish into the obscurity of time.

Looked at more closely, Brittany's memory is constructed of numerous superimposed and intersecting layers.

And though we know very little of the humans known as Teviec, who lived in the final phase of the last Ice Age, finding refuge from external attacks on the inaccessible rocky peaks, we know somewhat more about their successors who left extraordinary testimony of what were the most ancient European civilizations.

It was, indeed, in this region that the Neolithic civilization, which first appeared in the Balkan-Danube area, fully developed. It is in Brittany that its most evocative, even disturbing vestiges are found. Carnac, Locmariaquer, Barnenez are names as weighty as granite. Thus it was in a post-Romantic Europe, the recesses of whose territory was ransacked by armies of Celtic-loving "antiquarians," that the need was felt to baptize these dream stones that materialized from the lands of the Breizh with terms drawn from the language of Merlin, such as *menhir*, the tall rock; *dolmen*, the table of rock; *cromlech'h*, the circle of rock.

The people who probably arrived in waves from the steppes of southern Russia developed a matriarchal as well as sedentary society dedicated to agriculture. They left us megaliths among which the most ancient, the *cairns* and the *mounds*, primitive cupolas dating back to the 4th millenium B.C., were acquired from the Celtic culture together with the names of Ana and Cernunos.

These Neolithic populations were swept away but not annihilated by the Indo-Europeans, shepherds, warriors and worshippers of masculine, solar deities, who gradually spread throughout the territories of Europe between 4400 and 2800 B.C.

19 On the island of Gavrinis in the Gulf of Morbihan, a gigantic cairn or tumulus, was discovered by chance in 1832. It is one of the most splendid examples of the megalithic civilization that developed in Brittany in the 4th millenium B.C. The internal stone-faces are decorated with curvilinear motifs that call to mind those of Newgrange in Ireland.

20 Spirals and circles decorate these two pieces of pottery from the so-called Hallstatt period, a name given to the artistic/artisan production in the transition period between the Bronze Age and the Iron Age, between the 8th and the 5th centuries B.C. Pottery of Celtic origin abounds in homes as well as cemeteries. The variety of shapes and decorative motifs, for the most part abstract, allows for dating the pieces and identifying their geographic origins. Armorica produced not only many examples of stamped pottery but also magnificent vases with free-hand engraved decorations.

21 top Celtic tribes, fortified by their consolidated organization into classes and by considerable skill in metalwork, imposed their culture on the indigenous populations.

21 bottom left Initially inspired by Greek numismatics, Celtic artists quickly expressed all their originality and achieved a level of stylization that recalls modern art, as may be appreciated in this coin minted by the Cenomani in the region of Mans.

21 bottom center This coin, exhibited in the Rennes Museum, is attributed to the Armorican nation of the Namnetes, from which comes the name of the city of Nantes. The theme of the carriage, a symbol of the sun, recurs in all Celtic numismatics.

21 bottom right All the force of Celtic symbolism found expression in this coin minted by the powerful thalassocracy of Veneti in the south of Armorica. A kind of centaur led by a warrior adorned by a torque (a characteristic metal collar in use among the Gauls and later changed by the Romans) leaps onto a wild pig, a totemic animal of the Druid class.

The Celtic tribes of the second Iron Age, who belatedly arrived on these western promontories, profoundly influenced the local toponymy to the point that the words they introduced still resound in the names of cities such as Nantes, Vannes or Rennes, respectively Namnetes, Veneti and Riedones.

Around the independent Armorica, which probably included a part of Normandy and Maine, the actual territory of Brittany was divided into five nations, which, generally speaking, were Riedones to the east, Namnetes to the south-east, Veneti to the south, Osismes to the west and Coriosolites to the north.

Surprising monuments have come down from that age which an inexpert eye might confuse with the *menhirs* and which truly seem to have been made by the delightful Obelix! Round and low, slender, conical or cylindrical, smooth or grooved, these monuments called *lec'hioù* or Gallic stelae, are a testimony to the intense spiritual life of our forefathers. Dated between 450 and 250 B.C., they mark cemeteries where bodies or ashes were interred, two burial methods that were used concomitantly in Armorica. Ten of them can be found along the roads of Leon, isolated or in pairs, Christianized or not. Among these the most evocative undoubtedly is that of Sainte Anne, which dominates the beach of Trégastel. Sculpted with squiggles and vegetal designs, it is wisely attached to the complex of the Church of Plougastel-St-Germain. Until not very long ago, the girls of the village encircled this monument during the big procession (the *pardons*) in a ceremony which, in actual fact, had little to do with the Christian rites.

22 This 15th-century French miniature, which is filled with errors and anachronisms, depicts the naval battle between the Venetis' fleet, composed of true fortresses of the sea, and the galleys of Brutus, Caesar's nephew, off the coast of what is now Morbihan. The battle, which was turning in favor of the Armoricans, became a bloodbath when the wind fell.

23 In 56 B.C., Julius Caesar, the future dictator, seized on the pretext of the Venetis' detention of two Roman officials, to declare a vicious, bloody war on them.

Unfortunately, the independent Celtic civilization ended suddenly towards the middle of the 1st century B.C.

Caesar looked unfavorably upon the Atlantic commercial routes divided between the Armoricans and the Phoenicians. The Venetis' monopoly over the tin extracted in the Cassiterides Islands, which numerous authors identify with the Scilly Isles, the Sorligues of the French, irritated Rome.

Then, in the summer of 56 B.C., war broke out! The Gauls took refuge on inaccessible rocky spurs from which they were able to flee by sea whenever the Romans were sure that they could encircle them. After exasperating months spent in a vain attempt to entrap the indomitable Gauls, the future dictator decided to defeat them on the ocean. This was no easy task since the ships of the Venetis, compared to the fragile galleys of the sons of the she-wolf, were truly floating fortresses. That was true, but as such they were also very heavy. Fast under strong winds, they become cumbersome and not easily maneuverable in light winds. At the end of the summer, according to Caesar, misfortune or the gods, plagued the Venetis, their Armorican allies and the Bretons themselves. Off the shores of the Peninsula of Quiberon — and not in the Gulf of Morbihan, as 19th-century historians maintained — a naval battle raged. The Armoricans were winning. But the wind fell: Brutus' sailors surrounded the Venetis' ships.

With the aid of ingenious devices, they cut up halyards and shrouds and boarded the fortresses from the keels ... of clay. It was a bloodbath, a massacre to which Caesar contributed with his "legendary generosity," as Hirtius, his faithful secretary, would say. It ended with the extermination of the enemy leaders and the sale at auction of nearly half of the Venetis population.

But the courageous Armoricans were not, however, annihilated, and many of them found refuge on the island of Britain, in particular in the territory of the modern Wales, where they founded the counties of Gwyned and Gwent.

Subsequently a *Pax Romana* was established comparable, in certain ways, especially at the beginning, to a funereal peace. The crushed Armorica was annexed to Gallia Lugdunensis with which it would share its destiny for four long centuries. But is this truly romanticizing? If some authentic Roman cities emerged from the Armorican woods, such as Vorgium, now Carhaix, the entirety of the countryside remained, in all probability, Celtic-speaking. Can we believe Abbé Henri Poisson when he peremptorily said "the Armoricans were nothing other than Celts disguised as Romans"? Now, as then, it is useful to distrust pre-packaged ideas and theories. But since Roman poet Ausonius assures us that, in his family, living in Bordeaux, the Celtic language was spoken in the 2nd century A.D. and that it was still used in the region of Arverne well into the 4th century, there is reason to suppose that it long remained the idiom in use in the western promontories.

24 Was it the arrival of the Angles and the Saxons, as this 12th-century miniature shows, that "chased" the British toward the northern coasts of Gaul, in particular toward Armorica? According to Léon Fleuriot, the historical reality is much more complex.

25 Taken from a 10th-century Anglo-Saxon manuscript, this illustration shows a Viking long boat. The Vikings increased their raids along Breton coasts to the point of installing stable colonies on the island of Groix and in the region of Tréguier. In 919, under the leadership of Raghenold, the incursions changed into a real invasion, but Duke Alain Barbe-Torte defeated the invaders in the memorable battle of Plourivo and drove them from the city of Nantes in 936.

Beginning in the 4th century, new blood and energy came from the island of Britain to an Armorica by then tired, subjected to the pirates raiding from the northern seas, generically amalgamated under the name *Saozon*, the Saxons. The agony of the empire began with the attacks of the barbarians. In gestation was the new world from which modern Brittany sprang. We have long been pleased to promote the image drawn from traditional iconography, showing Britons fleeing from the Anglo-Saxon hordes in their leather coracles, belatedly coming to populate a nearly deserted Armorica.

According to La Borderie, "In this phase, the human presence in the Armorican peninsula was altogether accidental. The territory was infested with brambles, undergrowth and its ferocious inhabitants."

The reality is undoubtedly less definite. The Britons, who shared the same geopolitical environment as the Armoricans, often crossed the Channel to land in an Armorica that was not in fact totally depopulated, as La Borderie sustains.

They arrived there, at least initially, much more as protectors than as fugitives. In short, originally from the western regions, those who fled surrendered most probably to the pressure of the raids of the Scottish pirates or of the northern Picts rather than those of the Angles or the Saxons.

For our patriotic historian: "Without the Britannic immigration, the Armorican peninsula would have been a Latin-speaking region, a province of the Frankish kingdom, a languishing, uncultured, desolated country devoted to paganism." In this apocalyptic description, if you wish to credit these hagiographic accounts, probably only the latter statement is credible.

The Britons who disembarked en masse starting in the 5th century recreated the kingdom on the other side of the Channel, importing a new religion to the inhabitants of Armorica, who were still predominantly pagans. Together with their political leaders, the *tierns,* their priests, Malo, Indut, Brioc and Tudual, they created bishoprics, the *plou* and the *tre,* administrative and religious subdivisions that have been handed down to present times.

Here and there saints reputed to be such by the collective imagination, fought shouting and exploding fire-breathing dragons, as did Efflam, presumed cousin of King Arthur, on the shores of the Bay of Lannion. At their side, Gwenc'hlan, "the last druid," hurled his curses against the "foreign" princes and Christian priests who, having put out his eyes, threw him into an unending darkness. In the Bay of Douarnenez, the vulgar invaders assaulted the city of Ys. Unbeknown to Saint Gwendole and his father Gradlon, in search of strength and advice from the priestesses of the Isle of Sein, a beautiful, rebellious princess fled from the city, defying the power of the new spiritual masters of the country. From the mists of its origins a new country emerged, permeated by a dual historical memory, British and Armorican, and by a dual religiosity, Christian-Celtic and Druid.

25

Beginning in the second half of the 6th century, migration intensified. While on the island, the Britons of Ambrosius Aurelianus were subjected to Saxon assaults, which had by then assumed the proportions of a true invasion, Armorica first became Litavia and then Brittany. According to Léon Fleuriot, "In short, in a century, the number of Britons who established themselves in Armorica grew progressively until they had acquired political power ..., initially as *foederati* of the Romans, and found themselves the rulers of the country."

In the High Middle Ages, the country was divided politically into three distinct realms: Domnínée to the north, Cornouaille to the southwest and Bro Waroc to the south. In the clashing of sharpened swords, the assassins amounted to parricides. Brittany was still searching for its limits and the menace of the Franks was already on the horizon.

After innumerable attempts at annexation and a series of more or less fruitful incursions, in 818, Louis the Pious, the Carolingian emperor, succeeded in defeating the troops of King Morvan, who led the resistance from Poher. Brittany lost its independence. At least that is what the Franks thought. Then Nominoë Nevenoe, called Tad ar Vro (literally "father of the country"), the son of a noble, rich Breton family, was named governor. At the death of Louis, he freed the people of the obligations imposed and rejected restrictions and privileges imposed by the new ruler Charles, known as the Bald. Wishing to crush the "rebels" using decisive methods, after the signing of the Treaty of Verdun, which confirmed his reconciliation with his brothers, Charles undertook an expedition to Brittany. In November 845 — and not in June, as La Borderie and all the nationalistic school together with him insisted — at the head of an army, undoubtedly inferior to what Bertrand d'Argentré stated, he invaded Breton territory.

Unfortunately for him, the Bretons were awaiting him. Using light cavalry and throwing weapons, they avoided man-to man combat, re-introducing a strategy inherited from the *bagaudes,* peasants and soldiers who had rebelled against Rome. In the swamps of Bains-sur-Oust, they inflicted heavy defeat on Charles who fled villainously, abandoning his troops and the booty of war.

Important from the military aspect, the victory of Ballon was equally so from the psychological and political viewpoint. Freed from the threat of the Franks, Nominoë lost no time in organizing a true political Breton nation, run exclusively by people from there. According to Yann Fouéré, "In terms of its historical consequences, Nominoë's victory over the Franks is, in many ways comparable to that of the Scot Robert Bruce at Bannockburn over the Anglo-Saxon forces. Thanks to Nominoë and Robert Bruce, Brittany and Scotland were the only two Celtic nations to have a state organization in the modern sense of the term during the Middle Ages."

26 top Little Brittany has always been coveted by its powerful French neighbor, which constantly attempted to conquer it. In 497 Clovis, portrayed here in a 14th-century French manuscript, succeeded, annexing the region to the Franco-Carolingian kingdom.

26 bottom Louis the Pious, portrayed here in a 14th-century miniature, defeated the famous King Morvan in 818. In the same, disastrous year, he imposed Benedictine rule on the Abbey of Landevennec, which had, up till then, followed Celtic ritual customs.

27 In November 845, Charles the Bald attempted to annex Brittany. But the heavy French cavalry was massacred in the marshes of Redon by a highly mobile Breton army, equipped with spears and riding on the backs of small, fast horses. During the night, the sovereign villainously cut and ran.

28 Many Breton lords joined the army of William the Conqueror in 1066, believing they were going to free Brittany's islands from invasion by the Anglo-Saxons. As a reward, Alain le Roux, portrayed here, received the county of Richemont-Richmond from William, which later passed to the Breton duchies.

Nominoë, the *Tad ar Vro*, pushing the war into the heart of France, met his death at Vendôme in 851, but his work was carried on by his son Erispoé, who annexed the counties of Rennes and Nantes, later receiving the royal symbols. His successor Salomon conquered Avranchin, Cotentin and a part of Anjou.

For Father Chardronnet, "At Salomon's death, the Breton kingdom was at its apogee, which was, nonetheless, fragile." The Norman menace that hung as much over Armorica as Ireland ensured that the "more fragile" Brittany became the prey of these men from the north which devastated it under the scornful gaze of its French neighbors.

But, in 937, Alain, known as Barbe-Torte, inflicted painful defeats on the Vikings, first at Dol and then at Plourivo, initiating a period of stability to the west of Couesnon. But though having averted this danger from the north, the Breton sovereigns, who by then bore the title of dukes, had no respite in preserving the independence of the country. For several centuries they employed a shrewd policy of balance of power between their two powerful neighbors, the English and the French, who looked with interest on the little state, jealous of its independence and the influence that it hastened to acquire. Unfortunately the death of Duke Jean III left the duchy with no direct heirs, at the mercy of the rivalry between his brother Jean de Montfort and his niece Jeanne de Penthièvre. The two contenders appealed to the two foreign powers, Jeanne to France and Jean to England, once again placing the independence of Brittany at risk. After a forced exile in Britain, during which the French king, Charles V, brazenly announced the confiscation of the county of Brittany, Jean de Montfort triumphantly returned to Dinard on August 3, 1379, recalled by his vassals in this moment of danger. He was heartily welcome by the population, the memory of which was nourished by *Barzaz Breiz*. "Neventi vad d'ar Vretoned! Ha mallozruz d'ar C'hallaoued. Dinn, dinn, daon! D'ann emgann! D'ann emgann ho, dinn, dinn, daon, d'ann emgann a eann!" "Good news for the Bretons! And curses on the French. Our lord Jean is returning …. Din, don, dan, to battle, din, don, dan, I'm going to battle!" Once more freedom was preserved! Just in time. Beginning with the reign of Jean IV and that of his son Jean V, who succeeded him in 1399, the Breton navy underwent extraordinary expansion, reaching the point of rivaling that of the Low Countries.

While the Duke of Brittany, who still refused to render obeisance and fidelity to the king of France, flourished a crown as royal symbol, his powerful neighbor was preparing plans for attack.

28-29 This parchment illustration of the French School, dated 1472, shows a phase of the Battle of Auray, fought on September 29, 1364. This episode ended the Breton war of succession with the victory of the Anglo-Breton faction of Jean de Monfort over the Franco-Breton alliance of Charles de Blois.

29 bottom In the mid-1400s, English reinforcements disembarked in aid of Breton troops. During the entire period of their independence, the duchies of Brittany maintained a skilful diplomatic balance between their two powerful neighbors, England and France. The Breton army, defeated at Saint-Aubin du Cormier in 1488, included a contingent of 300 English archers.

Louis XI who ruled France from 1461 to 1483, continued to corrupt the great Breton nobility. And he succeeded to the point that it was those of the most noble birth, the Rieux, d'Avangour and other Rohan families that, in 1487, fomented a plot against their duke, François II, imploring the help of the French.

After a siege, the Breton army was defeated on July 28, 1488 near Saint Aubin du Cormier.

With the treaty signed on August 14th in Verger Castle, François II was forced by King Charles VIII to swear submission to him and to promise not to marry his daughters without royal consent.

When the duke died of heartbreak on September 9th of the same year, his daughter Anne freed herself from those contractual bonds. While Charles was once again attacking Brittany, she married Emperor Maximilian of Austria by proxy. Unfortunately, under siege in the city of Rennes and threatened by an implacable war, Anne, with her husband involved in fighting the Ottomans, was forced to yield to the requests of her torturer who, among other things, succeeded in annulling her marriage.

Charles died in 1499, after cracking his skull on the beam of a low doorway, and Anne was obliged to marry his successor, Louis XII, a totally self-serving marriage which, however, guaranteed Brittany a wide margin of freedom! But Anne was called to God in January 1514. Her daughter, Claude, who would have married Charles of Luxembourg, the fu-

30-31 This 19th-century painting by Gillot Saint'Evre depicts the marriage between Duchess Anne, daughter of Duke François II of Britanny, and the French king Charles VIII who, in 1491, had defeated Francis after a terrible war. However, according to the marital agreement Brittany maintained considerable autonomy, which would later be suppressed during by the French Revolution.

30 bottom Louis XI, King of France, portrayed here in a 15th-century illuminated capital letter, used every means possible to demand obedience from the Duke of Brittany, who had not totally submitted to him and who had the arrogance to wear a crown. Louis paid gold to some important Breton lords, eroding the ducal authority and preparing for Brittany's annexation.

31 Antoine du Four offered Anne his manuscript Lives of Famous Women, *a 1505 work. A woman of character, loved by the people, Anne of Brittany struggled all her life to maintain the freedom of the duchy. Her remains are now in the Cathedral of Saint-Denis in Paris but her heart stayed in Nantes until over-zealous revolutionary policies caused it to disappear.*

ture Holy Roman Emperor Charles V, was obliged to wed François de Angoulême, who rose to the Franch throne in 1515. It was the end of independence for the duchy because, while the Edict of Plessis Macé signed in Vannes in 1532 conceded, on the one hand, a certain number of rights to Brittany, among which was the withholding of taxes to France, on the other hand, it transformed a marriage of convenience into a perpetual territorial annexation.

32 Initially favourably received, the Revolution displeased Bretons because its leaders refused to abolish the tithe and the expiration of farming contracts. The ban on having sacred processions, the suppression of the rights of the duchy, the hoarding of "national property" by the bourgeoisie and, above all, the draft of 300,000 men, inflamed the countryside.

However, until 1789, Brittany, with the intermediation of its parliament and especially of its States, which had legislative duties, resisted all attempts by the king of France aimed at limiting its autonomy.

Two revolts, a popular one in 1674, called the "Stamped Paper" or "Red Berets," and another in 1719, that of Cellamare or Pontcalleck, of aristocratic inspiration, attempted to restore Brittany's ancestral rights, but they were suffocated in blood.

Tensions between representatives of the duchy and the central government were present, frequent and nearly permanent. But at the very least, the States succeeded in having the clauses of the 1532 treaty respected … until the fateful night of August 4, 1789 when the representatives of the Third Estate (the bourgeoisie) present at the Estates-General in Paris sacrificed the "privileges" of the "province" at the altar of ideology and an abstract nation, without even consulting the other estates which would, among other things, be suppressed the following year.

The end of autonomy, more than the execution of Louis XVI, and the continued attacks on religious freedom, together with the threat of conscription — the famous "draft of 300,000 men" — triggered the conflagration in a country by then already seething.

In March 1793, Brittany revolted, animated by a strong sense of injustice and laced, (because of intellectuals like the Marquis de la Rouerie), with federalist leanings. The revolt of the Chouans (local insurgents) led by courageous representatives of the people, conquered the countryside, conducting a war of attacks and ambushes until Napoleon finally captured the last Chouan leader, George Cadoual, and ordered his execution in 1804.

The Restoration in 1815 gave no recognition to this peasant army, always suspected of rebellion, hastening, instead, to consecrate a Bonapartist centralism and to ratify the suppression of the ancient provinces, something that the French kings had long desired.

Brittany no longer existed. It no longer had "documents." It was not even on the map. It had no name. It was nearly lost to memory. It was dismembered into five "departments", lacking in sense, history and social significance.

32-33 In 1795, the ineptitude of Count Hervily wrecked the landing of pro-Chouan reinforcement at Quiberon though the Bretons kept control over the countryside, this setback demonstrated the impossibility of communication between them and a nobility which only hoped to regain privileges.

In the ambitions of Parisian power, very soon it was not even to have a language any longer, persecuted by all the regimes that followed one another over the course of the 19th century which was obsessed by the ideal of cultural uniformity.

Its population, whose annexation had forbidden it outlets to traditional seas, had no choice but suffering or forced immigration to the capital where many young girls ended up as streetwalkers. The common people bowed down while the bourgeois "elite" integrated themselves with enthusiasm and servility.

But Paris distrusted the Bretons, rightly reputed to be less integrated than other peoples. Despite a bitter and ruthless struggle against the language suspected of threatening "the unity and indivisibility" of the "national" territory, on the whole the Bretons continued to use the last Celtic language on the continent.

In 1870, when the Prussians were threatening Paris, the young Republican government resorted to the draft. General De Keratry, a young aristocrat from Cornwall and ex-prefect of the Paris police, recruited a Breton army. Some 80.000 volunteers were given the task of stopping the German advance. Unfortunately Léon Gambetta, who combined the functions of President of the Council and Minister of War, obsessed by the specter of the "chouans" decided to abandon them in the camp of Conlie, near Mans with no cots for sleeping, no weapons and no food.

The Breton soldiers, victims of the cold and of typhus, died like flies in the tragic winter of 1870-1871. It was an army of ghosts, racked by fever and desperation, which on January 11th was sent to certain defeat in the "battle" of the Tuileries. It is understandable that this massacre, premeditated by the French government, deeply shocked the Bretons: M. Bidard de la Noé, mayor of Rennes, along with General De Keratry, Arthur Le Moyne de la Borderie and Count Le Gonidée de Tresson decided to resume Cadoual's struggle.

The poet of Morlaix, Tristan Corbière, dedicated the splendid *Pastorale de Conlie* to this tragedy, a song of enormous emotional charge in which he manifests his disdain for what his people endured.

The Brittany that lives, thinks and nourishes itself with the grand dreams of chivalric King Arthur is not dead.

In the wake of Théodore Hersat de la Villemarqué's 1838 publication of Barzaz Bretz, the "Kalevala" of the Bretons, a generation of authors, poets and writers worked on "Brittany material," laying the premises for the future. Meanwhile a sort of modern and romantic inter-Celtic movement arose.

At the end of the nineteenth century, a timid reawakening of political claims appeared with the creation of the URB (Union Régionaliste Bretonne) in 1898. It was animated by symbolic figures such as Régis de l'Estourbeillon, deputy of Vannes, about whom the folklore expert Anatole Le Braz, author of the renowned *Légende de mort chez les Bretons armoricains,* had written.

On the spiritual front, in 1900 at Guingamp, Taldir Jaffrenou, Yves Berthou and another twenty men of letters, after receiving the bardic investiture from their Gallic cousins, founded the Goursez of druids, bards and prophets of the peninsula of Brittany.

34-35 Prussian troops march on the Champs-Elysées in Paris after the surrender of the city. In January 1871, the French command sent the volunteers of the Breton Army, reduced by the inferno of Conlie, against the enemy units.

35 The Marquis Régis de l'Estourbeillon, deputy from Vannes, was the heart of the U.R.B. (Union Régionaliste Bretonne).

But, alas, the movement had just seen the light when the terrible First World War, 1914-18, began. It turned into a massacre for the Breton troops largely enlisted in the infantry and systematically sent to the front lines. If certain patriots like Louis-Napoléon Le Roux, the "Breton *Sinn-Feiner*," secretary to Padraig Pearse, head of the Provisional Government in 1916, preferred exile in Ireland rather than fighting and dying for the "invader," the "regionalist" intellectuals faithfully served France, nourishing the hope that when the "the war for peoples' rights" was over, their sacrifice would be repaid with a certain cultural, political and administrative freedom. Unfortunately, the delegation led by Commander Jacob and the Marquis de L'Estourbeillon, was not even admitted to the Peace Conference in 1919. The Bretons had, once again, fought another's war, a war in the interests of the others, for the right of others to decide for themselves, a right which, for the victors in 1918, was evidently not applied to Bretons or to their brothers in Ireland.

However, while once again Ireland arose against the abhorred Sassenach, a handful of young people, radicalising the positions of the *Emsav*, the Breton movement, created the *Unvaniezh Yaouankiz Breizh*, whose newspaper *Breizh Atao*, inspired by the Irish exam-

36 top left While their men, recruited first and used in the most dangerous sectors, put their lives at stake on the front lines, these women of Brest were exploited as low-cost workers for the war industry.

36 top right The illustration shows a truly idyllic scene. In reality, the First World War was a catastrophe for Brittany, which lost 240,000 of its sons in the trenches of Verdun and Dixmude.

36-37 Between August 3, the date on which the American tanks overran Rance, and August 25, 1944, the day on which they entered Concarneau, the Allies freed all the Breton territory. The German pockets of resistance in Lorient and Saint-Nazaire, however, stood firm until May 1945.

37 top This photograph, from June 1943, shows in what condition the city of Rennes found itself. It was the victim of tremendous bombardment near its station, which, in broad daylight on May 29, 1943, caused the death of 210 and the injury of 250. Brittany paid a heavy price for the war. The bombing of Nantes, on September 16th and 23rd, caused the deaths of 772 people and injuries to 1,775. The port cities of Saint-Malo, Saint-Nazaire, Brest and Lorient were almost completely razed to the ground.

37 bottom At Saint-Briac, in the interior of Saint-Malo, Bretons welcomed the Americans exultantly. But the hard times had not yet ended; ration coupons remained in use until 1947!

ple, did not delay in supporting national independence.

The attempt in 1940 by a minority to obtain from Nazi Germany the support that the Irish had asked for from the Kaiser in 1916 immediately gave the French government to repress all the Breton movements both cultural and political in the summer of 1944. But when the storm passed, under the form of musical and "folkloric" activities, Brittany began again to live, to breathe, to hope.

In 1947, Polig Monjarret created the first *bagad*, the Breton version of the *pipe band*, giving birth to a movement which, by mid-century, had acquired notable importance. In fact, in 1957, returning from Ireland, where a significant part of the *emsaverien* had found refuge, Dr. Yann Fouéré founded the MOB (Mouvement pour l'Organisation de la Bretagne), which claimed on the political level the rights that Joseph Martray and the CELIB (Comité d'étude et des intérêts bretons) claimed on the economic level. Indeed the Brittany of the 1950s, underdeveloped, hindered from autonomously administrating itself, victim of a downright social hemorrhage, seemed almost like a third-world country.

The "agricultural revolution" of the 1960s and 1970s made Brittany the leader of the European region in agricultural food production, making it possible for part of the population to remain and blocking the migratory flow, even though the Parisian ideological and technocratic rigidity still aroused mistrust and revolt.

38 bottom Immediately after the war, there was an extraordinary musical revival, embodied, in particular, by the bagadoù, *musical groups formed of some* binioù vraz, *or large bagpipes, eight* bombardes *and numerous Scottish drums. In 1947, the musician Polig Monjarret created the* clique *or band of the railwaymen of Carhaix, which, within a very short period of time, had many admirers.*

38-39 Breton agriculture went from the so-called archaic stage of the "Glorious 30s" to that of modern, intensive agriculture, inundating European markets with milk, cauliflower and artichokes. Now biological cultivation and a new farming culture are beginning to make themselves felt.

Both to impede the ill-timed land centralisation and to slacken the centralist hold, the FLB (Front de Libération de la Bretagne) appeared in 1966, gathering in its ranks representatives of all the social-professional categories. The symbolic attacks this clandestine organisation carried out had the aim of attracting the world attention to the fate reserved for the country of King Arthur and obtaining compensation from the French state.

Three decades later, the result seems somewhat modest.

If Brittany appears to be definitively past the condition of underdevelopment derided by the Parisians, the Breton "model" of intensive agriculture is increasingly criticized both within and without the region.

Brittany, indeed, has again found its name and a semblance of recognition of the administrative kind, especially after the Deferre law of 1982, which decreed election of the Regional Council through universal suffrage. And there are grounds for thinking that, if Prime Minister Raffarin's reform sees the light of day, the region will obtain broad responsibilities, bringing it closer to other European regions.

As for the population, which has been freed from the old inferiority complexes thanks to the cultural and musical renaissance that followed the Alan Stivell phenomenon, they dream again of a stronger and more autonomous Brittany, fully re-embracing the ancient claims of the *Emsav*.

39 right After the inauguration of the first Diwan associative school in Ploudalmézeau in 1977, teaching of the Breton language has moved forward. In 2002 Breton language schools had 7,682 students.

39 bottom "Brittany is Life" declares this banner around which are gathered, among others, the TV journalist Roger Gicquel, the singer Alan Stivell and the president of the Conseil Culturel de Bretagne, Jean-Louis Latour.

ARMOR: THE INHERITANCE OF THE SEA

40 top The high tides that can be seen in Brittany's waters, creating absolutely spectacular effects, are among the highest in the world, and ocean currents are particularly strong.

40 bottom Crozon is like a balcony extended into the sea, facing America. Those who have not had the good fortune to look from the cliff onto the Sea of Iroise, filled with the majestic fleet of traditional boats which sail from Brest to Douatnenez, cannot imagine the splendor of these waters.

A r mor, the sea. Can you imagine a fate more connected with that liquid immensity, its songs, its roaring waves, its nightmares than that in which 1250 miles [2000 km] of uneven coast stretches towards the chimerical Avalon as much as towards the very real Americas?

This land is confused with the ocean to such an extent that it even takes its name — ar mor, Armorica ... "the land surrounded by the sea." Everything is written in this name in which the echo of the waves that break against the rocks resounds, the name for an ancient and terraqueous world that, in the West, celebrates the perpetually renewed marriage between land and sea. A border world in which aquatic creatures, Ahès Dahud, followers of the goddess Morrigan and magical inhabitants of the abyss, organize wild witches' sabbaths, sometimes real disasters for the sailors encountered them. In all ages, the destiny of Breizh has been intimately, profoundly, viscerally, ontologically mixed with the ocean. This ocean, contrary to what the neighboring French believed, did not form a border but, rather, a formidable connection! On the other hand, wasn't the reign of Arthur perhaps two-headed, at least in the dreams of the Bretons and their literature?

Sailors' land from time immemorial, land from which, according to the ancient chronicles, the Irish monk Brendan started his second transatlantic journey to the Antilles in the 4th century. A land from which the fishermen of Trégor and Goëlo advanced as far as the coasts of the New World to fish for cod in the Middle Ages.

In the sixteenth century the descendents of Merlin and Vivian, in their 80- or 100-ton caravels sailed all the known seas, selling the wines of Bordeaux in Flanders, the fabrics of Lèon or the woad of Toulouse in England. This was the epoch in which the port of Penmarc'h armed a fleet of over three hundred ships which sailed all over Europe, an epoch in which Jacques Cartier of Saint-Malo found the source of the St. Lawrence River in Canada and in which the cartography laboratory of Guillaume Brousconi in Conquet supplied the most important navigators.

In the centuries that followed, if the annexation to France ended by depriving Brittany of part of its traditional outlets, its people did not stop advancing toward far-off horizons. Privateers such as Dugay-Trouin and Surcoff pursued the English enemy for the King of France, making that defiance the stuff of legend.

The heirs of these giants of the sea are nowadays called Riguidel, Kersauzon, Alain Gautier or Tabarly, one of the most capable skippers of all times, who was lost in the Irish Sea in 1997 aboard his mythical *Pen Duick IV*. It is not an accident that the major transatlantic sailing competitions, such as the famous Route du Rhum, depart from this peninsula which seems like "a balcony extended into the sea" (Xavier Grall).

40-41 The sea has always shaped Bretons' lives and imagination. This photograph shows the Bay of Quiberon where, in June 1795, a considerable contingent of immigrants attempted to join the Chouans led by Cadoual for the purpose of restoring the monarchy and the freedom of the country.

41 top For many people, Brittany has become a synonym for recreation. The country of Eric Tabarly, Jacques Cartier and Dugay-Trouin continues to attract sailing enthusiasts, whether they use the older cotton sails or modern ones made of highly technological materials.

42 top When he comes back into port, the fisherman sorts the shellfish by size. In order to preserve this important resource, very strict laws require shellfish of less than 4 inches (10.2 cm) to be thrown back into the sea.

42 center A man installs a dredge which will allow him to gather molluscs from the seabed, separating them from the sand and mud.

42 bottom After harvesting, the molluscs are packed into sacks to be sent to auction, to be sold to the highest bidder.

42-43 Of the 17,000 people enrolled in the list of French fishermen, as many as 10,000 are Bretons. Those of the Bay of Saint-Brieue specialise in netting capesante, molluscs which once were little appreciated and which now instead find favor with chefs and gourmets.

But the ocean not only represents the search for individual affirmation; it is also the humble, daily adventure of anonymous heroes who rise before dawn to go to work on the immense watery expanse.

And though the days are over when the fishermen left from Paimpol, Binic or Saint Malo, pushing into the icy inferno of the northern Atlantic to fill their nets with cod, the great ocean still supports thousands of Breton families.

Looking more closely, out of about 17,000 French sailors, more than one-half are Bretons! The Armorican fishing haul on average amounts to 45% of the national total, and 50% of the manpower involved in the art of fishing are Bretons.

Aware of the immense potential wealth of the oceans, the Bretons launched new activities generating considerable added value, such as thalassotherapy or harvesting algae. The latter, with an annual production of 70,000 tons, already involves 3,000 laborers in the production cycle.

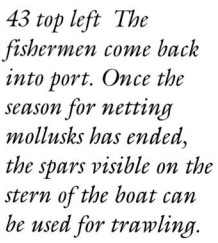

43 top left The fishermen come back into port. Once the season for netting mollusks has ended, the spars visible on the stern of the boat can be used for trawling.

43 top right With the winch, the fishermen lower one of the two dredges that will allow them to take as much as 1320 lbs (600 kilos) of molluscs in half an hour.

43

44 bottom A large French military port, Brest preserves some pleasant medieval vestiges. One of these is its 15th-16th century castle, now home to the maritime prefecture and the Naval Museum. Another is its 16th-century Tanguy Tower, shown in this photograph, on a sheer cliff over the military port, which now holds an interesting Museum of History.

44-45 The Albert Louppe bridge, inaugurated in 1930 by Gaston Doumergue, then President of the Republic, connects the austere Léon with the smiling Cornouaille. Since 1994, the connection has been doubled with the opening of the Pont de l'Iroise.

45 top, left and right Inaugurated in 1990, Océanopolis, at the entry to the tourist port of Moulin Blanc, is a vibrant homage to Lir, the Celtic god of the sea. A place for discovery, tourism, pedagogy and scientific research, it attracts about 600,000 visitors a year. With 1 million gallons salt water and its 320 employees during the summer season, this imposing complex consists of three pavilions, one for each of the climatic zones — temperate, tropical and polar.

The sea surely represents the future, a precursor of which is the Océanopolis Center which opened in Brest in 1990 and attracts more than a million visitors a year. Yet it also represents the memory of an entire populace. What would the sea have become if it had only been populated by monsters with outboard motors or if the last exemplars of the traditional wooden sailboats had ended their existence rotting in naval cemeteries? But so that this extraordinary patrimony would not be irremediably lost when

44 top Brest pays particular attention to its legacy of wood, hemp and cotton. Every four years, this city, an urban version of the more compact, intimate Douarnenez, hosts thousands of sailors from all parts of the world.

formica supplanted oak in the construction of beds and sideboards, a tiny group of enthusiasts, supported by the magazine Chasse Marée, decided to organize nautical events devoted to classical boats. What great strides have been made from the Pors Beac'h gatherings at Logonna Daoulas in 1980 to the extraordinary sea-fest in Brest and Douarnenez in 1996 which attracted over a million enthusiasts of wooden hulls! Indeed the movement was not limited to the organization of events; it also gave birth to the awareness that safe-guarding the maritime tradition is as important as handing down music played on instruments such as the Breton bagpipes *(biniou)* or the Celtic harp. Now from the Fête des Vieux Grèements (Festival of Classical Boats) in Ploumanach to the *Chants de Marins* (Sailors' Songs) festival in Paimpol, an entire patrimony is being recovered. In the Bay of Lannion, a traditional trawling net has been reconstructed. In Brest harbor, there is the *Recouvrance*, a faithful replica of a schooner from the beginning of the nineteenth century. In Odet, the lugger *Corentin* can be admired. Great is the wonder when, in the sparkling light of a summer morning, one of these venerable boats appears on the open sea with its dark cotton sails!

Ar mor, the sea. Imagine a land set on an unusually changeable coastline, in a shoreline from which the tide recedes, revealing a border world with the scent of iodine and of other worlds!

The coastline extends into infinity. The skies can change ten times a day with the *gwalarn*, which wails from the north-west, and the *reter*, which compete for the horizon. It isn't surprising that Plutarch pinpointed the landing stage for the *Tir na n'Og* precisely here, the place in which the courageous meet to have drinking sprees, where the cider and the mead run like rivers and where maidens have soft, welcoming thighs that offer repose to the warrior.

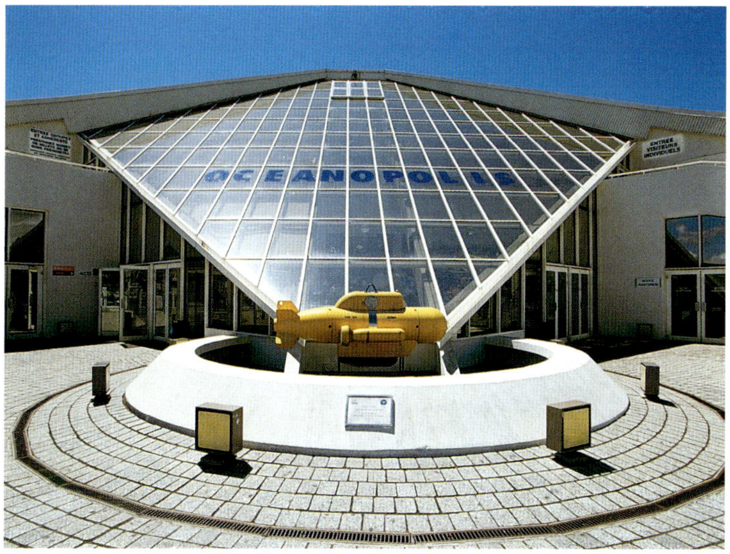

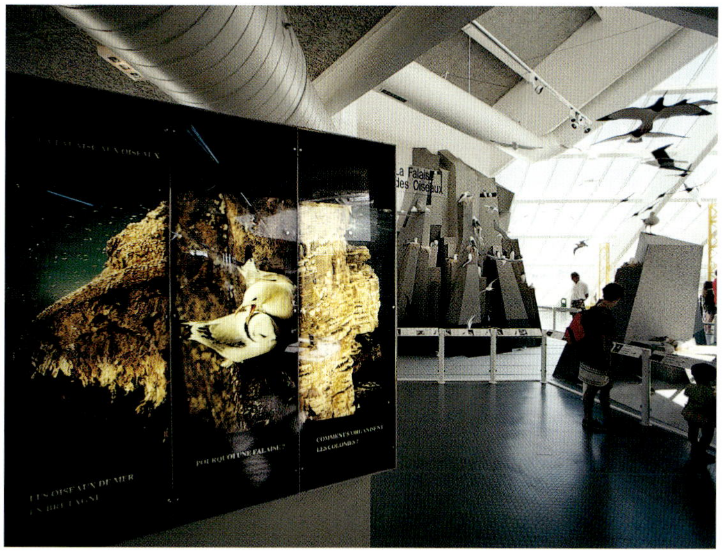

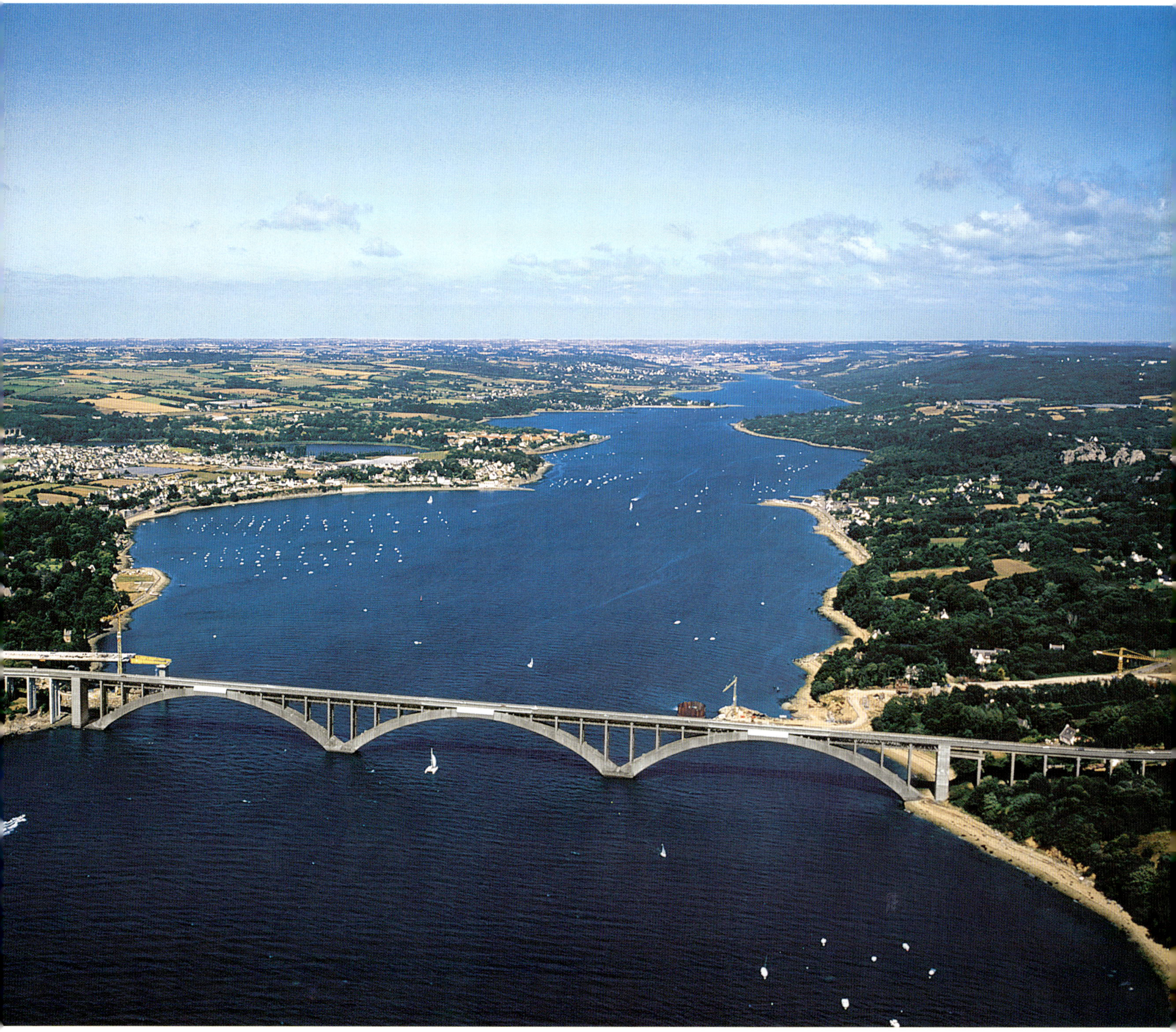

46 bottom Port-Anne on the coast of Vannes, pays respectful homage to Saint Anne, patroness of Bretons and, through her, to Deva Ana, the great Mother of the Celts and the gods, who continues to be venerated under the vestments of the Christian saint.

46-47 "Brittany is a universe" affirmed the Provençal poet Saint-Pol Roux, who made his home in Camaret. It was also he who defined Crozon as a muse "with a bonnet of indefinite outline" because of the enormous number of inlets and promontories.

47 top left At Pointe des Poulains, Belle-Île en Mer has cliffs that are among the highest in Brittany. To fully appreciate this wild, tortured coast, you have to see it swept by the waves during the equinoctial storms.

47 top right The southern coast of Brittany is a more gentle, colorful universe, less hostile than that in the north. It is an ideal area for nautical recreation, swimming and long walks.

46 top Considered by Plutarch as the departure point for the afterlife, Brittany remained such for centuries. The spectral vag-noz, the boat laden with the souls of the drowned waiting to be judged, crosses the Bay of the Departed.

Three bodies of water contend over the territory, making of this *penn ar bed*, the "head of the world," a crossroads and an extraordinary place of exchange. To the north is the Channel, to the west the Iroise or Celtic Sea and to the south the immensity of the Atlantic. An almost indecent variety of landscapes!

The north is an almost uninterrupted succession of high cliffs scarred by the Bay of Saint Brieuc, a deep cove in the bodice of Breizh. The eastern part presents points and capes and a cross-shaped peninsula, a kind of giant sea monster snoozing between the harbor of Brest and the Bay of Douarnenez. The south is a symphony of delightful small estuaries, a rosary of small harbors surrounded by cluster pines in which multi-colored boats float.

"Brittany is a universe" eruditely proclaimed the Provençal Saint Pol Roux, who knew what he was talking about. And it's true. And it's also true for Breizh, which begins here, at the edges of the immense bay of Mont Saint Michel, which, according to the old saying, "Couesnon in his folly placed in Normandy." An immense desert of sand and water in which the scent of the giants gently wafts. Wasn't the Mont perhaps called Gargan before being providentially Christianized, and doesn't the Isle of Tombelaine still remember the time when its name was "Tombe Belen"?

This is the region of excesses, an area in which, the inhabitants of the place assure us, the sea rises at the speed of a galloping horse! This suggestive image was quickly desecrated by the scientists who nonetheless recognize that, with a rise of over 53 feet (15 m), the tides of this area are the most accentuated on the planet after those of the Bay of Fundy (New Brunswick), Canada.

Cancale is famous for its oyster dishes and its *bisquines*, large albatrosses made of wood and cloth that enthusiasts of traditional sailing built in such great numbers that they could race with their Granville neighbors.

47

48 and 49 Mont Saint-Michel was, without a doubt, the ancient site of a Druid cult. The Ilot de Tombelaine, on which it rises, corresponds to the ancient Tun-Belen, "altura (sacred to God) Belen." It is an ode to the sacred that unwinds through a universe of immense proportions. Almost entirely located in Breton territory, despite the fact that the Mont itself is in Normandy, the Bay experiences tides among the most notable in the world, second only to those in the Bay of Fundy in Canada. The water recedes for over 12.5 miles (20 km), revealing a desert of sand where only those who know its secrets can venture.

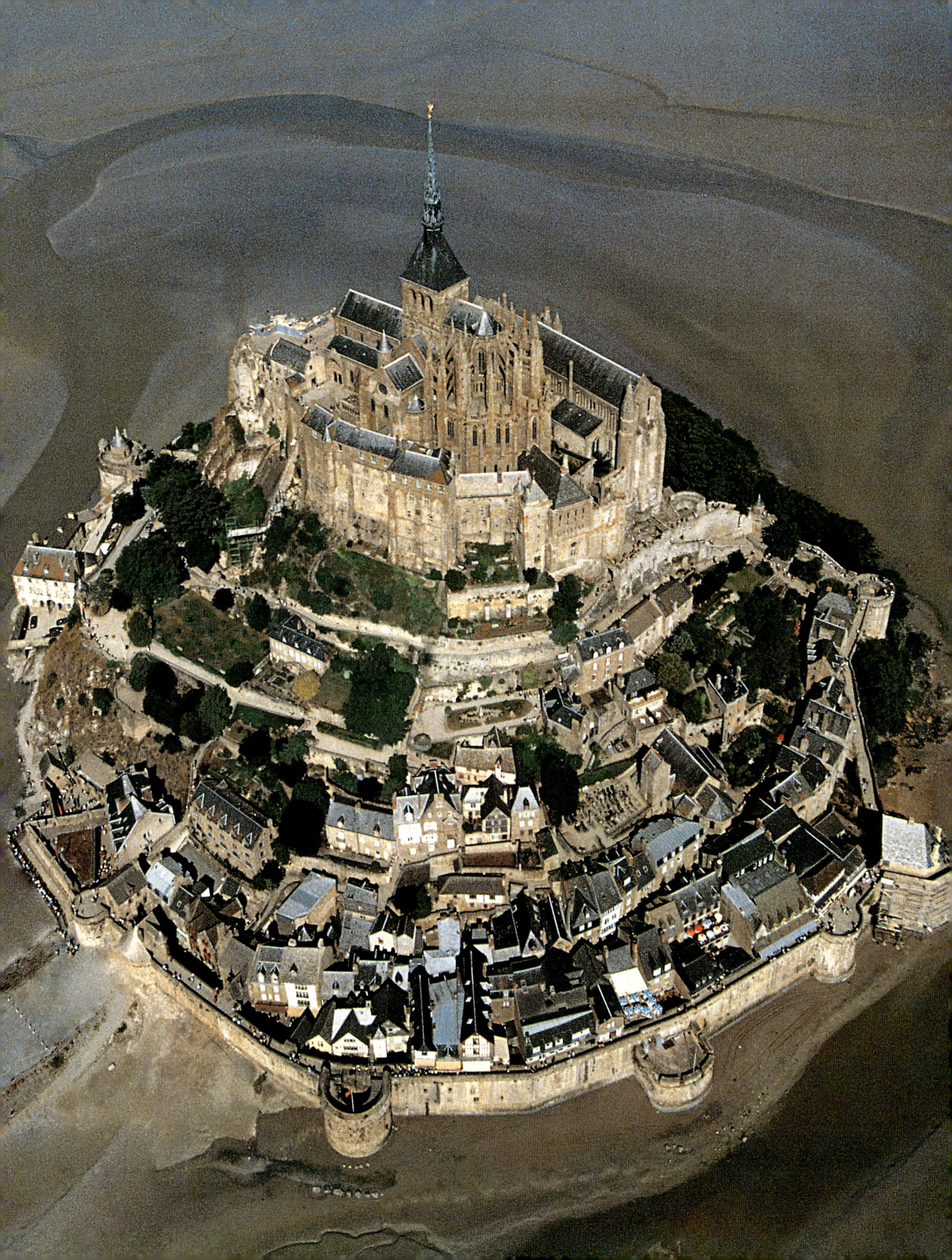

1,52 €
la Dz.
M4
3,04 €
la Dz.
M3
3,65 €
P5
2,14 €
la Dz
M4
3,04 €
la Dz.
M3
3,65 €
la Dz.
G2
3,35 €
la Dz.
1 Douzaine
GRATUITE
Pour l'achat de
5 DOUZAINES
à emporter

50 top left and right As early as the 4th century the Gallo-Roman poet Ausonius sang the praises of Breton oysters. Their fame has not diminished over the centuries — and the annual production of the dozen or so principal farms reaches 15,000 tons.

During low tide, the oyster farmer (left) with a tractor goes to the farm on the estran facing the bay. The oysters are then put into highly resistant plastic bags (right), with capacities up to 27 lbs (12 kilos), set on wide, iron shelves, and sold at three or four years of age.

50-51 Direct sales make it possible for the oyster farmer to double his earnings. Oysters are sold on the basis of their size. The average, labeled M3, which weigh between 2.7 and 3.0 oz. (65 and 84 grams), are generally the most valued.

51 top Cancale continues to be the undisputed Mecca of mother-of-pearl oysters. Its fame goes back to the 16th century and now a large number of gourmets gather there under the banner of the Confrérie des Hôtes de la Baie de Cancale.

51 bottom In this stock basin where they are tidily arranged in boxes, oysters can stay for weeks, waiting to be sold.

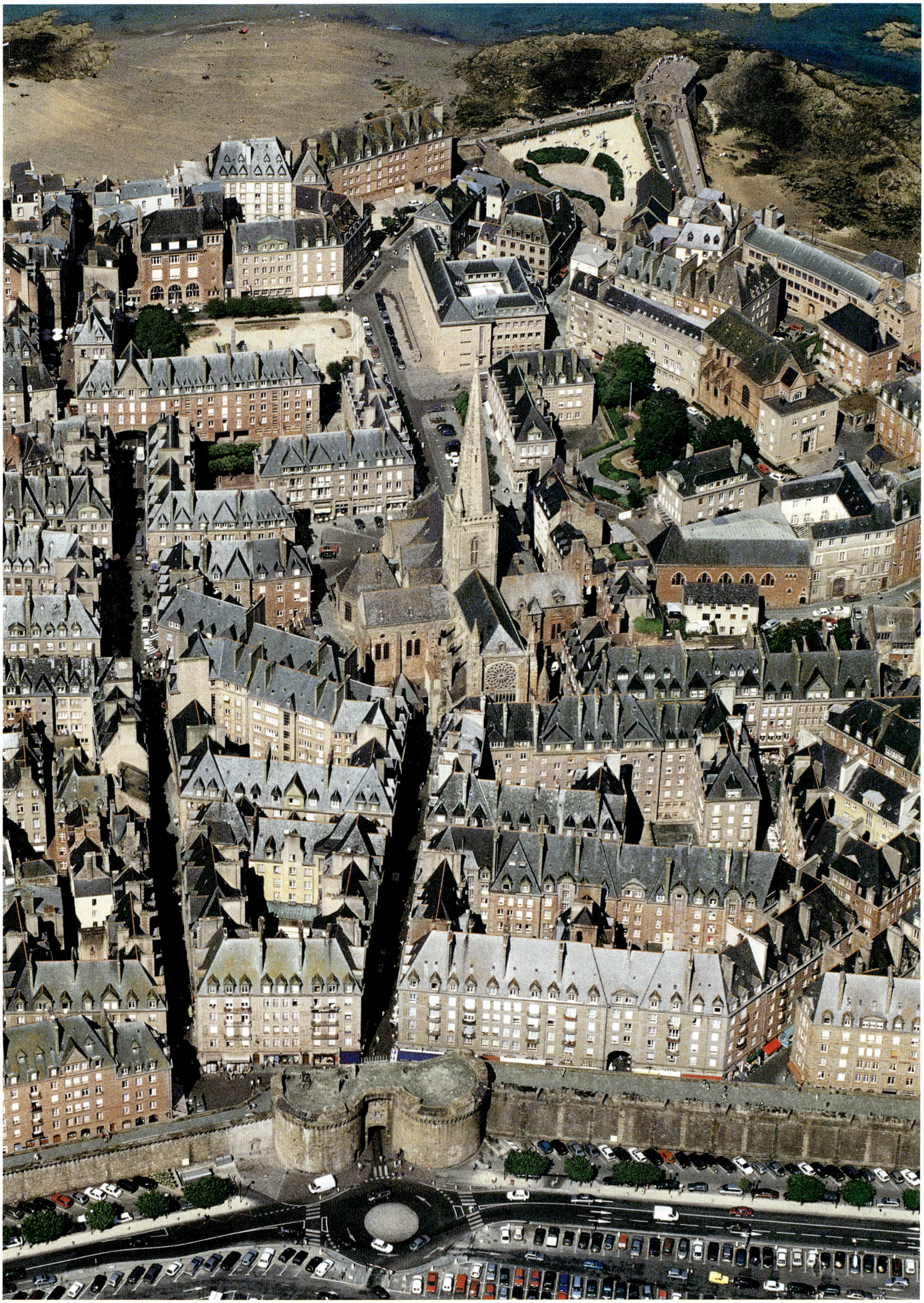

52 Destroyed by General Patton's bombardments, the city of Saint-Malo, with its wealthy dwellings, was faithfully — or nearly so — reconstructed right after the war. However, the bell tower of the cathedral was completed only in 1972.

53 left The city within the walls preserves the atmosphere of other times when the sailors made the famous "silk way" resound with their laughter. These iron fishermen symbolise the city's historical connections with the New World.

53 top right On the bottom of the ports of Dinan and Saint-Malo, the waters of the Rance are barred by a powerful dam that runs for a good 830 yds (750 meters).

53 center right, the photograph top François-René de Chateaubriand, originally from Combourg, wished to be buried on the island of Grand-Bé. For the Celts, this island is a place of initiation and rebirth, a visible fragment of the afterlife.

53 center right, the photograph bottom As the poet Xavier Grall forcefully wrote, in Brittany it is not rare for "the sea to defy the coast." The daily destiny of Bretons who live on the sea does not spare the proud descendents of pirates.

53 bottom right Over the years Saint-Malo has succeeded in making cultural, intelligent tourism prosper.

At the mouth of the Rance, guarded by the Solidor tower erected in 1382 by the highly suspect Duke Jean IV, rises Saint Malo whose motto "Malouins first, Bretons perhaps, French, if anything remains" reiterates dreams of independence. These dreams took shape at the end of the 16th century, marked by crime and blood, when, following the example of Venice, Saint-Malo proclaimed itself a republic. The leading port in France in the 18th century, the city still exudes the air of faraway places and the memory of sailors such as Dugay-Trouin, Surcouf, Mahe de la Bourdonnais, who initiated commercial activities in the East Indies, and Jacques Cartier, who explored north of the Indies — the West Indies. Now the sumptuous India cloth and even the acrid odor of the cod unloaded in enormous quantities on the docks of the port until the 1950s are nothing but a memory. Some 80% destroyed by the raining of General Patton's bombs in 1944, the walled city was never again constructed exactly as it had been. Yet the walk along the walls in front of the Grand Bé, where the last dwelling place of François-René Châteaubriand rises, is something unforgettable.

54

54 top left and right Behind its powerful bastions, the wealthy dwellings, rebuilt between 1947 and 1855, are a vibrant testimony to Saint-Malo's golden age when, in the 17th century, the city's ship owners developed flourishing trade with the Indies and the Americas.

54-55 Behind the bastions fortified by Vauban, behind the ancient walls of the beautiful city wed to the ocean, are told memorable adventures on the high seas.

55 top Saint-Malo and Portsmouth, UK are connected by Brittany Ferries, an efficient service founded by Alexis Gournevece, a local entrepreneur, in 1972.

56 top Brittany has always been — and still is — the synonym of space and freedom. The estran, *the stretch of coast abandoned twice a day by the sea, is a border world that allows for the most wonderful escapes.*

56 bottom This chapel of Saint-Michel rises on a small island near the village of Sables d'Or le Pins on the Côte d'Emeraude. During week-ends it is the preferred destination of families who gather mussels trapped among the shingle and rocks of the beach and exposed during the low tide.

56-57 Fort-la-Latte, the Gouyon-Matignon castle, a stone sentinel guarding the Bay of Fresnaye and, in the distance, the city of Saint-Malo, move romantics and the film-makers. It was here that Richard Fleisher shot the most evocative scenes of the film The Vikings *(1958), interpreted by Kirk Douglas and Tony Curtis.*

On the other shore of the Rance estuary, in the Dinard seaside resort, time stopped in the crazy years in which colonies of wealthy Englishmen and American millionaires went to dance the Charleston between a cocktail and a dip in the sea, wearing striped bathing suits. The 1929 crisis saw this mirage vanish while Camille le Mercier d'Erm, founder of the first P.N.B. (Breton Nationalist Party), insisted on maintaining the autochthonous presence.

Cap Fréhel is a long finger of shale and porphyry which takes on a blood-red color, skimmed by the light of the sunset. A cliff 230 feet (70 m) high jealously guards the mouth of the Rance and does it so well that, one fine day, the Gouyon-Matignon family decided to build this improbable citadel which juts out into the sea, a sort of surrealistic castle extrapolated from a Bernard Louédin painting. The film director Richard Fleisher was not mistaken in setting some of the scenes from his film *The Vikings* here, in particular the duel on the tower between Tony Curtis and Kirk Douglas, perfect in the role of that character. It was also here that Philippe de Broca shot the last scene of his excellent *Chouans* in which a lively Sophie Marceau plays an exuberant, aristocratic young woman in love and Lambert Wilson plays a military leader disturbed by abstract ideas.

57 top left The Fréhel lighthouse dominates dizzying red porphyry cliffs, which seem to be on fire at sunset. Built in 1950 at approximately 340 feet (103 m) above sea level near an earlier lighthouse erected in 1695 by the architect Simon Garangeau, it has one cyclopean eye that reaches for 29 nautical miles.

57 top right Dunes are environmentally delicate areas. To protect the plant species that grow there, the Conservatoire du Littoral has often been obliged to limit access to the dunes.

58 top Although golf has not yet acquired the fame in continental Brittany that it enjoys in Britain, it is now one of the most practised sports. The Saint-Briac course combines the green of the grassy carpets with the scintillating blue of the Channel.

58 center The Chapel of Saint Maurice, isolated in the greenery and crowned by the intense blue of the Bay of Saint-Brieuc, testifies to the religious feeling of a people who, at the dawn of the Middle Ages, followed with fervor the Irish and Gallic "saints" in leather-clad boats.

58 bottom The port of Dahouët, at Pléneuf Val André, after experiencing the golden years of cod fishing, is now specialised in capesante. The eastern end of the immense Bay of Saint-Brieuc, there is an ideal area for long walks.

58-59 To the west of the Bay of Saint-Brieuc, Binic, the pearl of the Armor coast, recalls the time of deep-sea fishing when, between 1612 and 1913, its elegant schooners sailed as far as the New World and Iceland in search of cod.

Flaubert was too sententious in peremptorily stating in his travel diary, a literary genre in which 20th-century writers excelled, "Saint-Brieuc: zero!" If it is true that the large village promoted to departmental chief town from the Revolution is boring in the monotony of a bay invaded by greenish algae, which are a nightmare for coast-dwellers, the extremities of the small bay enclose places of great interest. This is the case with Dahouëto to the east, the docking port of the launch *Pauline,* which found glory thanks to a song by Guillemer. O di Binic to the west still looks back on the propitious days of cod fishing when, in its port, floated the colorful boats specialized in fishing for Saint Jacques oysters.

59 top Despite its reputation, Brittany is not a land of mists and rain. Light and colors are often vivid and brilliant. And, as the locals, say, the weather is beautiful several times a day, as this view of the port of Binic, north of Saint-Brieuc, shows.

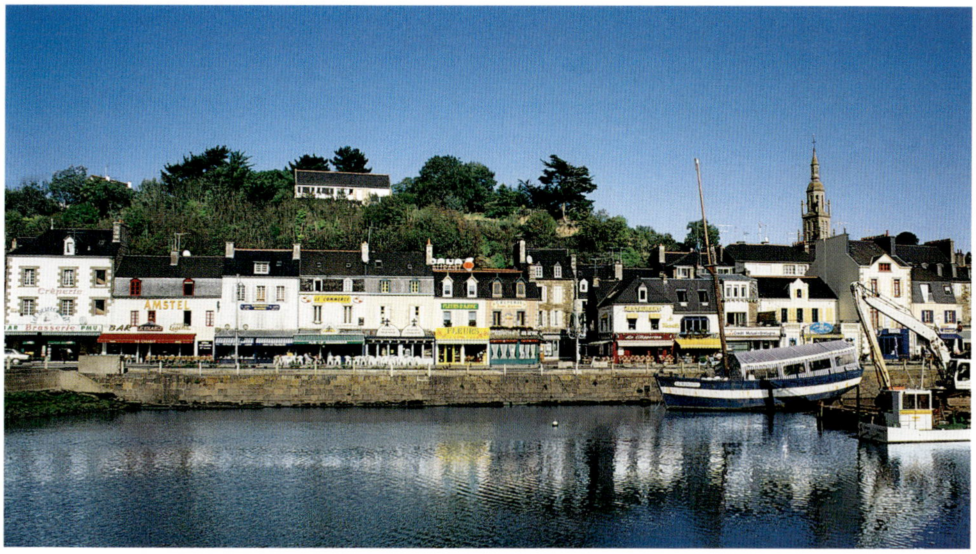

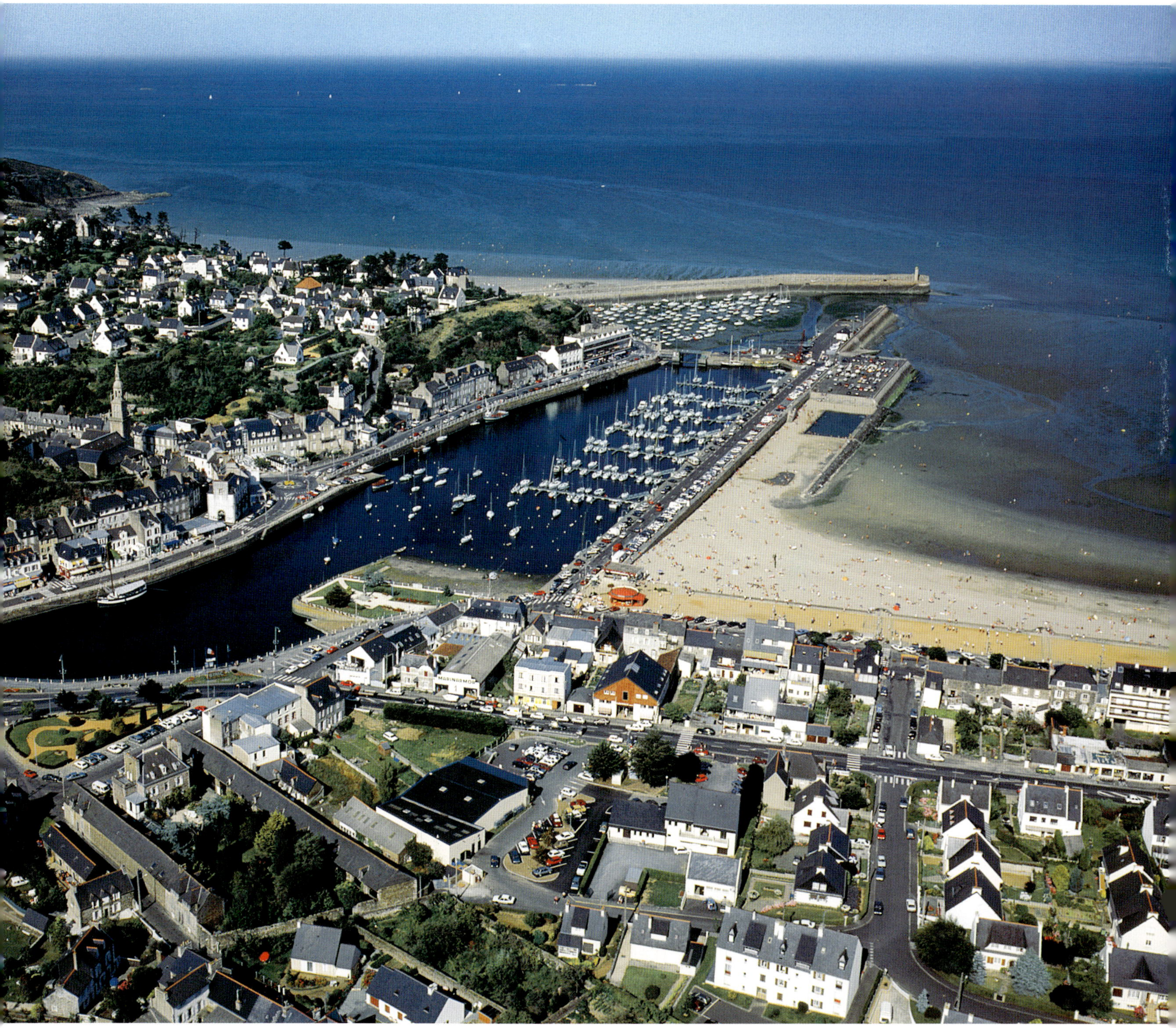

60 top Meadows studded with broom dominate the inlet of Bréhec, on the coast of Goëlo. This coast, among the most spectacular in Brittany, should be visited by following the coast road that winds for several miles ending at the enchanting Bilfor Point and the Minard.

60 center The most characteristic rock of the island, a beautiful pink granite much appreciated as a building material, abounds in the area surrounding the Paon lighthouse.

60 bottom More than an island, Bréhat is a true archipelago. With lacy rocks that glow at sunset, it was the refuge of inspired anchorites such as Maodez and Rion, before becoming the land of cod fisherman in the high Middle Ages.

60-61 The Bay of Paimpolis is a source of enjoyment both for connoisseurs and for simple visitors. In the distance, the St.-Rion islands and the Bréhat archipelago, refined pink granite lace, shine in the luminous blue of summer.

It is more to the west, past the Bréher cliff, that the magic begins. Paimpol never boasted of a cliff except in the mediocre song of that Montmartre fun-maker Théodore Botrel, who needed a rhyme. A short distance from Paimpol, however, the heavy stones of the Abbey of Beauport still preserve the memory of deep-sea fishing when, in the Middle Ages, the abbey imposed taxes on the cod caught in the north Atlantic off the shores of the New World. In good weather, the abbey comes alive to the rhythm of story-telling recitals and Celtic harp concerts.

On the route for the scattered archipelago of Bréhat, a stop at Ploubazlanec is an almost obligatory ritual. Here you find the cemetery of the sailors who died off the shores of Iceland in an epic tale that more closely resembles a punishment. A cemetery? The shadow of a cemetery. Names, thousands of names written with white paint on wooden tablets painted black — the names of all those boys of the land who, between 1853 and 1935, paid a heavy tribute to the great devourer.

61 top In the inlet of Kerity, the Beauport Abbey, founded in 1202 by Alain d'Avaugour, Count of Goëlo, celebrates quadruple marriages amidst stone, water, flora and Breton culture. This is a fragile, delicate balance that Laurence Meiffret, its director, makes efforts to maintain, to the great satisfaction of Korrigan, a reclusive cat who guards the place, the Ouessant rams and Shetland ponies that graze in its field.

61

62 top Brittany, as free-time culture would demand, is also a paradise for dilettantes, who fish standing on the estran or from small boats, nearly all of which nowadays have plastic hulls.

62 center During the good season, the southern part of the island of Bréhat, more inhabited and less wild, is often flooded by the rays of the sun. This is the kingdom of the agapanthus, the geranium and the hortensia — a true feast for the eyes right from the beginning of spring.

62 bottom A region influenced by very strong tides, Brittany has understood how to take advantage of this. During the Middle Ages, it boasted of the largest concentration of mills activated by the movement of the waves. In 1993, the commune of Bréhat entrusted the Birlmot Mill Association with the task of restoring the then neglected but magnificent building erected on the side of the Kerpont canal.

62-63 The name Paimpol is permanently connected with cod fishing, which had its moments of glory — and tragedy — between 1850 and 1930 when, during the summer period, adventurous schooners left the shore to capture fish off the shores of Iceland.

63 top Though more small-scale and diversified than on the southern coast, fishing continues to be very important in the northern part of the region. With an annual catch of 10,000 tons, of which crabs are a significant part, the fishing port of Paimpol is the most important in northern Brittany, second only to that of Brest.

Off the point of Arcouest extend the long pink lace rocks of Bréhant, a town whose sons were once destined to become sailors and which now has been massively converted to tourism. Though in winter almost all the shutters facing the large ocean are bolted, in the spring, the beautiful island begins to smile, murmur and rejoice again. It comes alive to such an extent that the only motor vehicles that can circulate are the small tractors of the islanders. In May, to the delight of the senses, the pastel blue of the agapanthus, the yellow of the mimosa, the pink of hortensia and the brilliant red of the geraniums are mixed together.

It is not surprising that inspired anchorites, such as Maodez arriving from (Great) Britain in his leather coracle, chose this little paradise to build their first monasteries.

Passing Lézardieux, you can ascend the Trieux estuary by boat or by the train that goes from Guingamp to Paimpol up to the Castle of the Roche-Jagut, a proud Breton mansion of the 15th century. It was purchased in 1958 by the Coasts Department, which dropped the adjective "north" to become "of Armor." Here you enter into the deep Trégor.

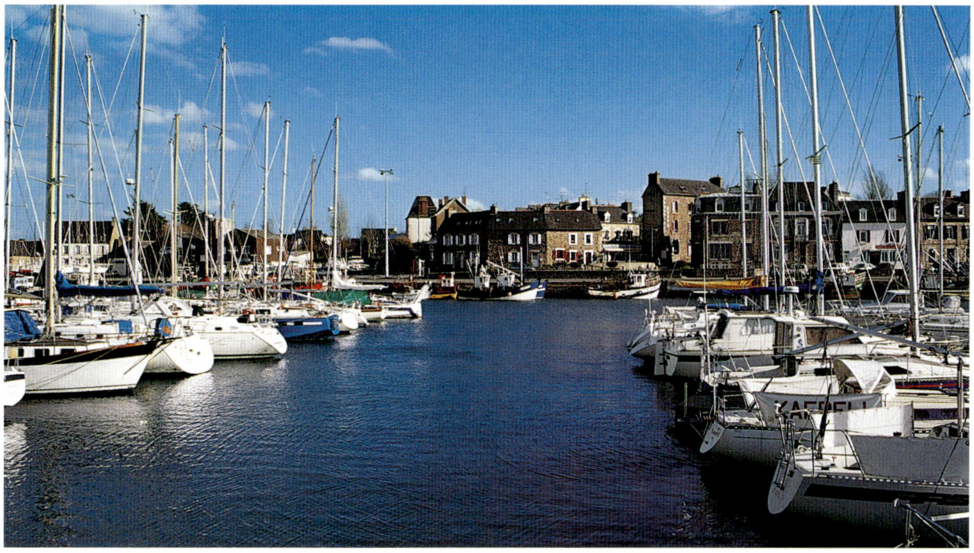

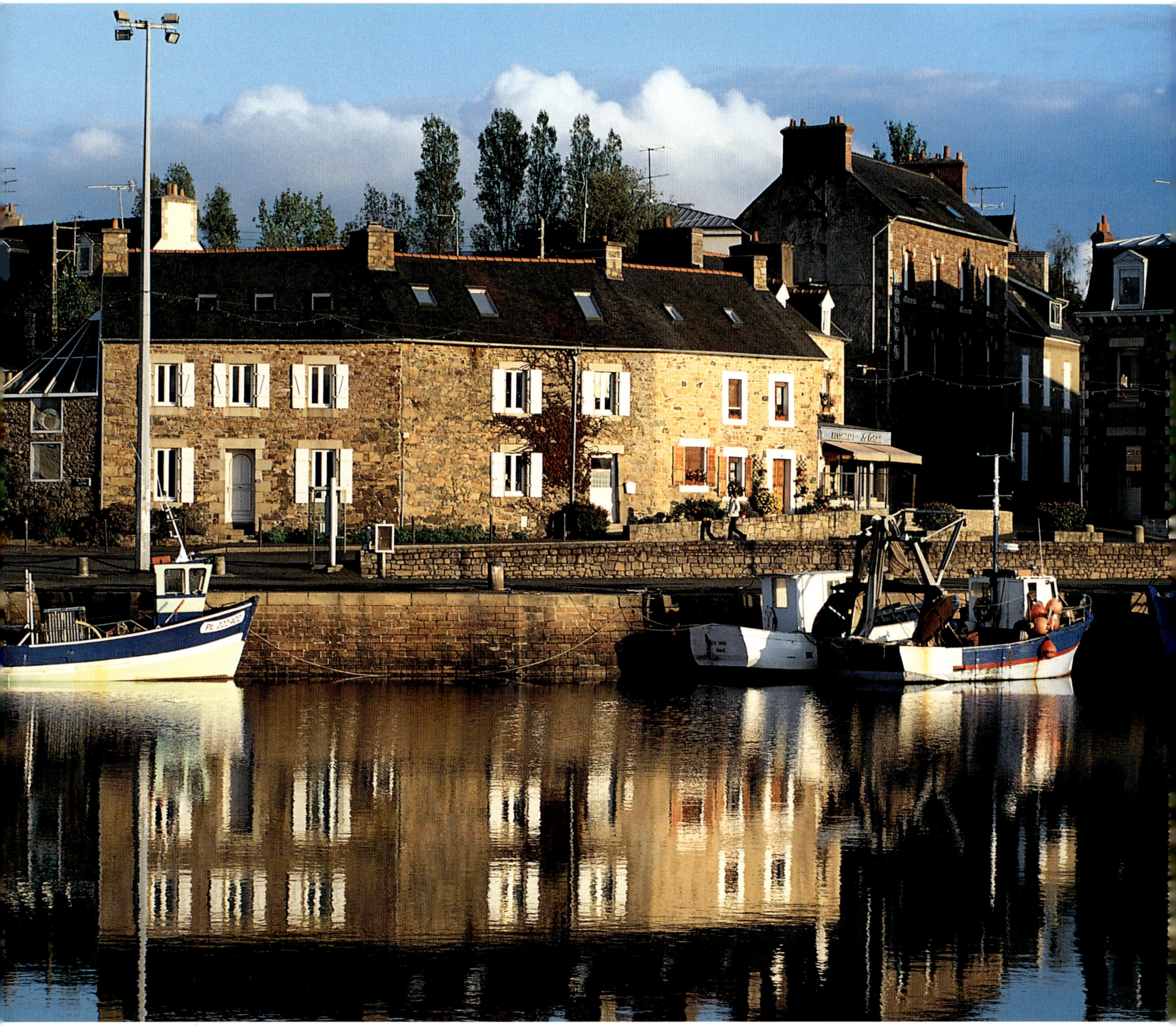

64 top and center Guingamp, on the border between Argoat and Armor, is a large city with medieval charm. The main square, with its famous Plomée fountain, is one of the most sumptuous in Brittany.

64 bottom The austerity of the stone is exalted by the enchanting contrast with the colored frames of this typical dwelling on the Côte d'Armor.

64-65 The Roche-Jagu castle in Ploezal, built on a bend of the Trieux in the 15th century, is the emblem of Breton castles. Property of the Conseil Géneral, the building is open to the public in the summer. Exhibits of a good level on various subjects, from the bagpipes of Europe to the history of Brittany, can be admired there.

65

66 right Along the Pink Granite Coast, houses built with this material with slate roofs have supplanted the old cabins. However, case, they are almost always harmoniously integrated with the landscape.

66-67 Lighthouse Point at Ploumanach has become the symbol of the famed Pink Granite Coast. On summer evenings, it is enjoyable to breathe the clean, iodine-rich air, lingering in the area of the Oratory of Saint-Guirec, on the customs officers' path, which winds in front of the Seven Islands archipelago.

67 top A little kitsch, a little surrealistic, delightful villas on the Pink Granite Coast date back to a time when the coast was not yet under the control of the Conservatoire du Littoral.

And here, in Pleubian communal territory is the Talbert peninsula, an odd finger of gray pebbles almost 3 miles (5 km) long pointing towards England and swept by storms nine months out of twelve. Then there is the extraordinary maelstrom of Penvenan, Buguélès and Plougrescant. Rocks, an infinity of rocks, skimming the water as far as the eye can see, rocks that make this coast a nightmare for sea-faring people. Going farther, between Perros-Guirec, which awakened at the beginning of the last century covered with flowering villas, and Trébeurden stretches the Côte Granite Rose. Here you can see almost surrealistic sculptures made from gigantic blocks that flame in the light of the setting sun next to the Ploumanach lighthouse or the neo-Gothic folly of Costaérès, where the Polish writer Henryk Sienkiewicz, a Noble prize winner for literature, withdrew at the beginning of the last century to write his *Quo Vadis*. We find ourselves in the heart of Trégor, the "Attica" of Brittany, the land of the bards, the land of Gwenc'hlan, "the last druid" who cast his spells — and his curses — from the top of the Roc'h Allaz precipitously down into the Bay of Saint Efflam. It is the land of the blind Hervé, canonized by *vox populi*, patron of bards and eponym of the little chapel that crowns the Menez Bré, the highest peak in the diocese.

66 left To the casual visitor, the heavy granite masses that run along the coast between Perros-Guirec and Tréburden can appear to be precariously balanced, but they strenuously resist the wind and salt water. The locals have practically adopted them and have baptised them with the oddest names.

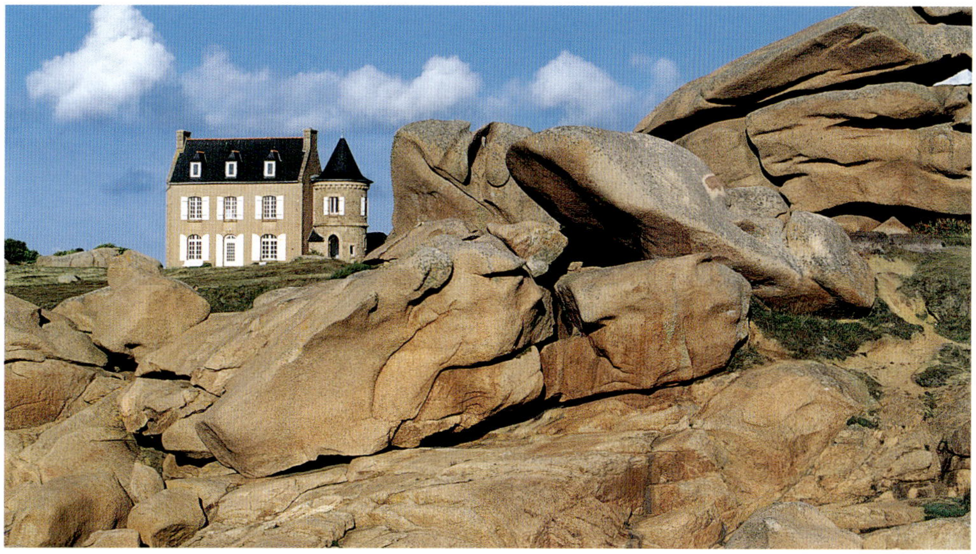

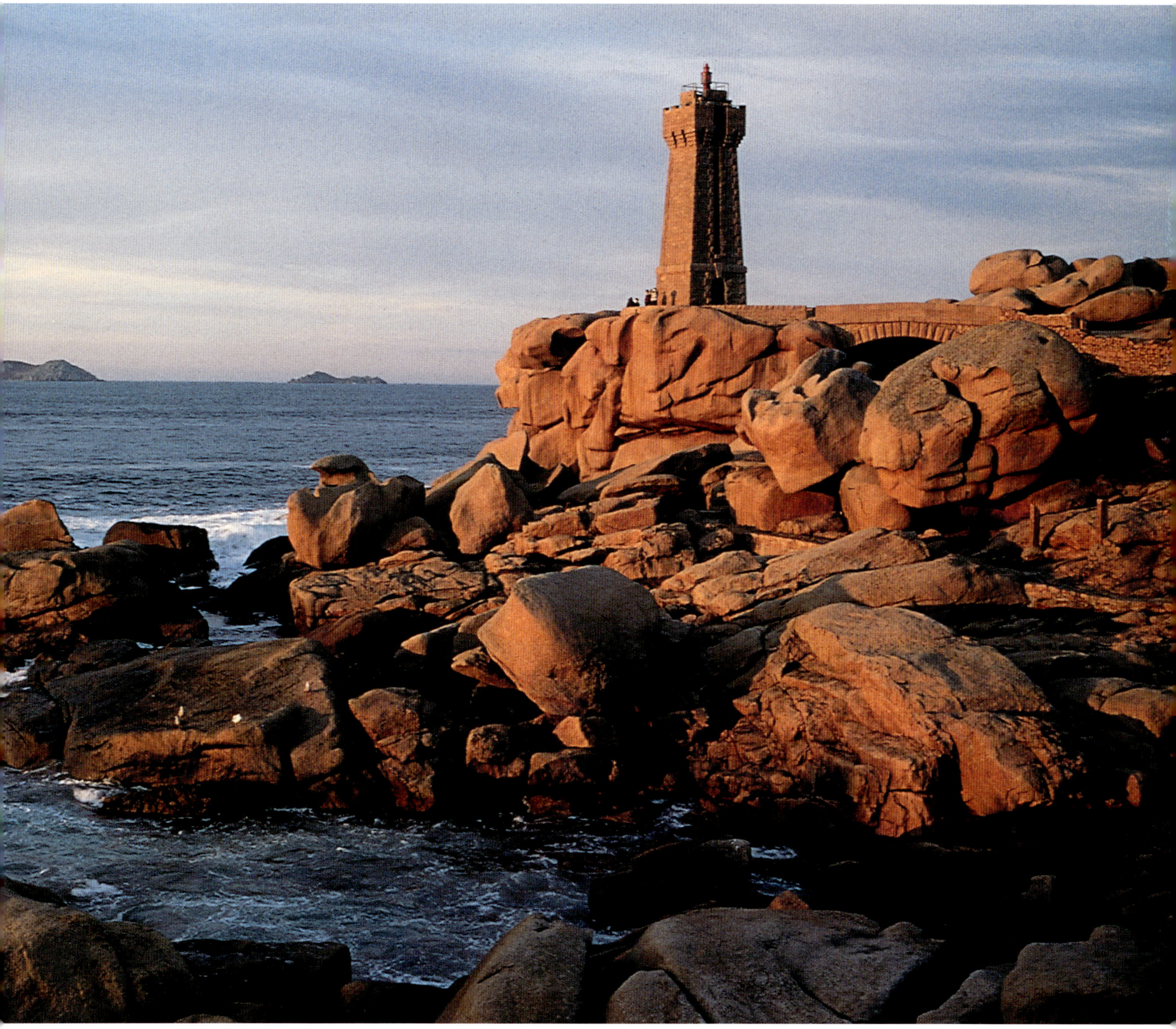

BOULANGERIE

68 top left In the port of Tréguier, the drakkers led by the fearful Viking leader Hasting have now given place to peaceful recreational sailboats.

68 top right On rue Colvestre, a road that leads from the Cathedral of Saint-Tudwal to the Arch Theater, stone buildings from the 17th and 18th centuries and rush-mat houses line the street. To better appreciate the fascination of this beautiful city, visit it in the summer, for the famous Tréguier Wednesdays, when the smells of sardines and barbecued pork spread through the streets.

Anatole le Braz, author of *La légend de la mort chez les Bretons armoricains* loved to withdraw into his small cabin in Penvenan. And it was in a rush-mat house in the old Tréguier, episcopal seat until the Revolution, that the philosopher Ernest Renan was born. These places resound with the history of entire generations. Don't the Ancients say that it may have been on the Isle of Aval, that scarf of sand off the shore of Pleumeur Bodou, that King Arthur sank into sleep, watched over by his step-sister and lover Morgana? And in the sound of the waves on the Lieue de Grève, which casts its magic spell near Mont Saint Michel, don't attentive ears perhaps hear the faraway echo of the fight between the Irish Efflam and the horrendous dragon which terrorized the land?

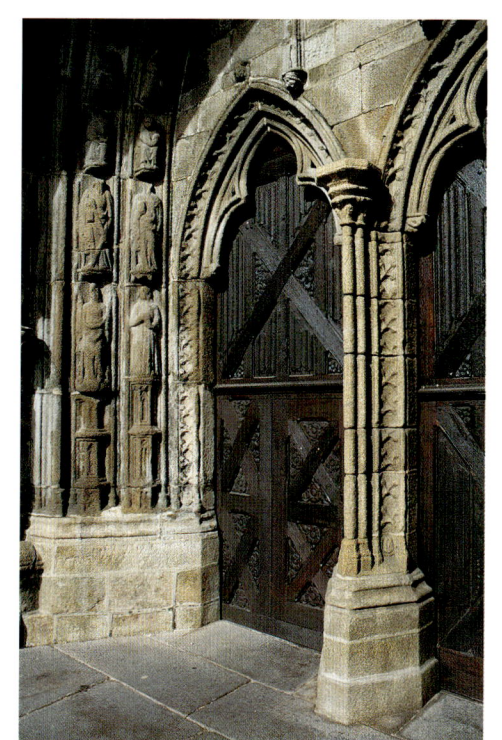

68-69 The episcopal city of Tréguier which, it is said, was founded in 532 by Saint Tudwal, one of the seven saints who founded Brittany, underwent significant economic, cultural and religious development between the 13th century and the French Revolution. Place du Martay and the rush-mat houses that watch over the statue of the philosopher Ernest Renan are a legacy of the city's golden years.

69 top right Ernest Renan, along with Yves Helori de Kermatin, is Tréguier's most important native son. He was born in 1823 in a splendid rush-mat house on the street that now bears his name and died in Paris in 1892. He is the author of the immortal Recollections of My Youth, *a work that faithfully portrays the soul of his people.*

69 bottom left and right The Cathedral of Saint-Tudwal, built between 1339 and the end of the 15th century, houses the tombs of Saint-Yves and Duke Jean IV. It is one of the most lavish churches in Brittany. Its cloisters, in particular, are a marvelous example of Flamboyant Gothic architecture.

70 top The coasts of Brittany are still a paradise for marine birds, at least for those whose populations were not decimated by the oil spills that darkened the coast.

70 bottom Rocks abound on the northern coast of Brittany and only the most expert sailors can venture into these insidious waters. This photograph shows the entire Seven Islands archipelago.

70-71 The solan goose, this albatross of the northern seas, with a wing span of 6 feet (1.8 m), is one of the bird-symbols of the Seven Islands Reserve, a few miles to the north of the Perros-Guiree beach.

71 top left The Seven Islands Ornithological Reserve also hosts several dozen gray seals — the only colony in Brittany along with that of the Molène archipelago — which like to lie on the rocks covered by goemon algae during the low tides.

71 top right Rouzic Island, closed to visitors, is the only French sanctuary of the solan geese, which, in the springtime, come by the thousands to build their nests.

Only fifteen minutes to the north of Perros-Guiree is the Seven Islands archipelago, at one time the hide-out of pirates and monks, now super-controlled and classified as an ornithological reserve since 1912.

With the single exception of the Île aux Moines, the archipelago, now forbidden to human visitors, is the uncontested domain of the penguin torda, the guillemot, the Dougall tern, the solan goose, the albatross from the northern seas, the crow and the puffin, which succeeded in surviving the slaughter provoked by Parisian "hunters" at the beginning of the twentieth century and the subsequent black tides, among which the most terrible was that of *Torry Canyon* in 1967. With a bit of good fortune, you may happen to see some of large gray seals from the local colony stretched out on the rocks.

71

72

72 top Enez Louet, "the grey island," north-east of the vast inlet that forms the Bay of Morlaix, is a familiar shape to those who are accustomed to walking on the coast. Behind it is Taureau Castle, built in 1552 to protect the city from the raids of the detested Saozon (the English). It served as a prison in the 19th century and as a sailing school in the 20th. A clear sign of the times!

72-73 Near Primel Point, the western end of the Bay of Morlaix which dominates the inlet of the Deben and the lobster harbor of Primel-Trégastel, enormous granite masses have pink reflections that recall those of Ploumanac'h. The route beyond the village of Saint-Jean du Doigt, either on foot or by car, offers absolutely unforgettable scenery.

After passing Locquirec point, whose Sables Blanches beach was the scene of the unusual military landing organized by the EMSAV (the movement for Breton autonomy) on the eve of World War II and the impressive rock formation of Dibenn, which drops sharply into the harbor of Primel Trégastel, you enter the Bay of Morlaix, celebrated by the writer Michel Le Bris who settled there. This is undoubtedly one of the most extraordinary bays of Brittany. Just in front of the little seaside resort of Carentec, there is the Île Louet, with a lighthouse that looks like an exclamation mark. Taureau castle hindered the arrival of the hated Saozons (the Breton name for the English) in Morlaix. The castle was used as a prison and it is said that it held famous prisoners, such as the revolutionary Blanqui, before it ended its career, more prosaically, as a sailing school. On the hills of Plouezoc'h is the cairn of Barnenez, six thousand years old, in part dismantled in the 1950s by a not very scrupulous businessman and now protected by the Fine Arts.

73 top The Bay of Morlaix, dominated by the Barnenez cairn and watched over by the elegant, noble residences of the ship owners and the pirate captains of the 18th century, is one of the most extraordinary ones in northern Brittany. It was in these waters that the poet Tristan Corbière, author of the immortal collection Amours Jaunes, loved to sail aboard his cutter with cotton sails.

73 center and bottom At Trégastel, the island of Renote is separated from the mainland only when the tide is at its highest. In this world of earth and water, where granite and the light prevail, it is difficult to distinguish between land and sea.

74

74 top left The Abbey of Saint-Mathieu, at the northern tip of the Brest harbor and a few miles from the port of Le Conquet, was founded in the 12th century by Benedictine monks who had the reputation of dividing the spoils from the terrible wrecks of those ships from "pagan countries."

74 top right Roscoff, "the old pirates' cove" written about by Tristan Corbière, has, since 1973, been an important port which represents a traité d'union *between Great Britain and Ireland. The departure of the ferry for Cork, each Saturday evening, is somewhat like a voyage of initiation.*

74-75 Just 15 minutes from Roscoff, the island of Batz is a little paradise in which agapanthus, hortensia and mimosa grow abundantly. Contrary to what occurred at Bréhat, it has been able to keep its population at home thanks to fishing and gathering of seaweed.

Léon's coasts are undoubtedly less remarkable than those of Trégor. As for their inhabitants, if you want to believe what their neighbors to the east say sarcastically about these "cauliflower sellers" and other "Prussians of Brittany," they may be less extraordinary but that does not make them less authentic. For example, the Île de Batz, which faces Roscoff, "the old pirate hideout," dear to the poet Tristan Corbière, allows a population of 650 souls to live thanks to fishing, gathering seaweed and especially producing vegetables, among which are excellent organic potatoes.

Léon is a marvelous land of *abers*, aber Wrac'h, aber Benoît, aber Ildut, which make the coast from Portsall to Brignogan resemble the Norway of your dreams. Its inhabitants, however, assure you that it is only malevolence that attributes to this "Bro Pagan" (pagan land) a reputation as a pirate hideaway, even though the annals of the Abbey of Saint Mathieu, located on the cape of the same name, attest to the fact that the monks had the right to a tenth of what was found in wreckages.

How many recollections are hidden in the mists of a memory that is sometime unsound and often sad. Now that the great fear of the black tides, such as that of the *Amoco Cadiz,* which in 1978 spread crude oil over 250 miles (400 km) of the coast, is over, people are going back to the sea to live. Now, however, it is the gathering of seaweed, which makes up 80% of the French yield, that is a reason for pride for these pagans.

75 top The economy of the island of Batz, along with fishing, has given ample space to the production of early produce.

75 bottom The western coast of Léon is marked by deep, spectacular inlets called aber, *a name found in the spoken languages in Brittany, Wales and Caledonia. A residue of ancient glacial valleys, they are the fjords of Brittany.*

75

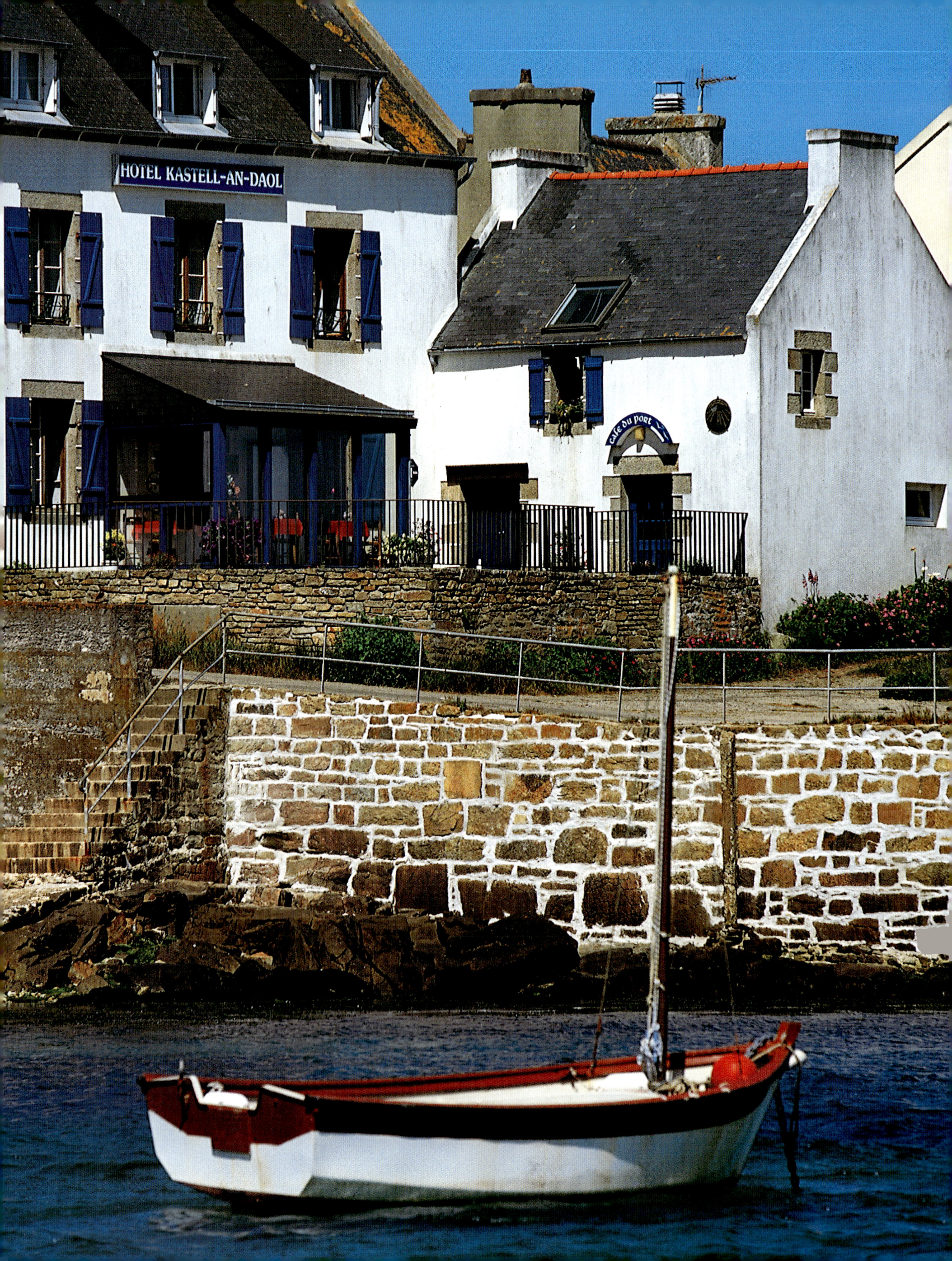
HOTEL KASTELL-AN-DAOL
Café du Port

76 The Hotel Kastell-an-Daol, in the microcosm of Molène, is a world apart, a place not to be missed. One has to have spent an evening in the restaurant managed by Erwan Masson and a night cradled by the lapping of the waves on the pier to have a sense of a marine paradise.

77 top This house respects the building canons of Ouessant toward the end of the 19th century. It is a building of about 40 x 20 feet (12 x 6 m), with two rooms on the ground floor, the penn brao *or nice part and the* penn-kuizin *or the kitchen. In contrast to what occurs on the continent, the furniture on the island of Ouessant, often made with wood taken from shipwrecks, is harmoniously painted in blue and white.*

77 bottom left The wild coast that forms the western side of the Île d'Ouessant between the Pointe de Pern and the Creac'h lighthouse is a mesmerizing environment which offers a unique spectacle during winter storms. The emotion is such that one almost expects to see the magical creatures of the abyss emerge.

77 bottom center The Creac'h lighthouse on the western coast of Ouessant, completed in 1863, was the most powerful in the world at the beginning of the last century. Its large cyclopean eye now has the task of watching over one of the most crowded routes, a true highway of the sea.

77 bottom right The Molène archipelago, with its painted wooden houses, vaguely brings to mind Iceland or the Färoës. Stone, however, is the dominant material in its traditional architecture and slate has now replaced straw for roofs.

The west is the land of fear. The names of its islands and its promontories sound like so many assurances of drowning. This is a hard and hostile environment bordering on the savage, often mixed with something of the supernatural. It is an environment which, as a reaction and as a necessity, the people have woven a net of mutual solidarity.

But is the Ouessant, the Uximana of the Pytheas, the Greek navigator, who was also called "the very tall," a land of humans? Rather it is a desert of minerals where trees do not grow. It is where, until not very long ago, people slept in homes with furniture made from flotsam wood painted blue and white. It is where homes were heated with a strange combustible mixture made from goemon and dry cow dung. It was where the proper functioning of social life was entrusted to the women with long, dark, flowing hair who, what's more, claimed the right to ask for the hand of the man they had chosen! Now the large eye of the Cyclops Creac'h, lovingly kept by Théo Malgorn, lights with its yellow ray, the longest in the world, the terrible "course" of the Ouessant, a sort of lane into which each day about a hundred iron giants crowd, their bellies filled with black, poisonous blood.

Off the shores of Molène, the current of the Fromveur roars like a monster from the deep, among the ghosts of the drowned people from *Castle Drummond*. Meanwhile, from his tabernacle in the Castle in Daol, on the island celebrated for the enchanted piano of Didier Squiban, the great warlock, Erwan Masson, dispenses sparks of life and heat.

78 top The Bay of Dournenez, one of the most extraordinary in Brittany, should be visited in the height of summer when it hosts an armada of period boats of every kind and size: luggers, bisquines, chasse-marées and coracles.

78 bottom According to an ancient legend, the vag-noz, "the boat of the night," would slowly cross the Bay of the Departed weighed down by the souls of drowned people. For this reason, it's not a good idea to linger around here.

78-79 La Pointe du Raz was declared a Site of National Interest in 1989. Off the coast of these impressive cliffs against which the ocean waters foam, between the continent and the Île de Sein, exceptionally violent currents rage.

79 top Sein is only the appearance of an island. A comma of land, stone and seaweed, situated on the sea as if by magic, it is a rough world where one has daily to resist the wild assaults of the sea. According to what legend tells us, here the beautiful, rebellious princess of Ys, Ahès-Dahud, unbeknownst to her father Gradlon, went to consult the nine Sènes, the last priestesses of the Druid religion.

To the south, between Cap du Raz and the Île de Sein, which, at 5 feet (1.5 m) above sea level (at its highest point!) has often been submerged by infuriated waves, the "raz" is face to face with hell. "Whoever sees Ouessant sees his own blood," according to the saying, which hastens to add, in an impetus towards equality, "whoever sees Sein sees his own end," just to be welcoming. Brrrr …! We should not be surprised if our forebears, sharp observers, always in direct contact with the back of the mirror, had located in this reassuring comparison the famous Bay of the Departed, in which the *vag noz* docks, "the boat of the night," loaded to the brim with the heavy souls of the drowned. Nor that Anatole Le Braz, letting his imagination run wild, chose the Vieille lighthouse as the setting for *The Guardian of the Fire*, the most macabre of his novels. In this novel, the guard Goulven Denez imprisons his woman and her presumed lover in a room in the lighthouse with a chamber pot as the only piece of furniture and witnesses their interminable agony with morbid pleasure. Neither is it surprising that, exactly in the middle of the sumptuous Bay of Douarnenez, popular imagination situated the submerged city of Ys, the city that the princess Ahés Dahud, the fiery daughter of King Gradlon and Woman from the Other World, built with the help of the populace. Passing the Pays Bigouden, where at the dawn of the 20th century maidens still did suggestive fertility dances around phallic stones and rounding the point of Penmarc'h, the "horse's head," the south offers completely different landscapes.

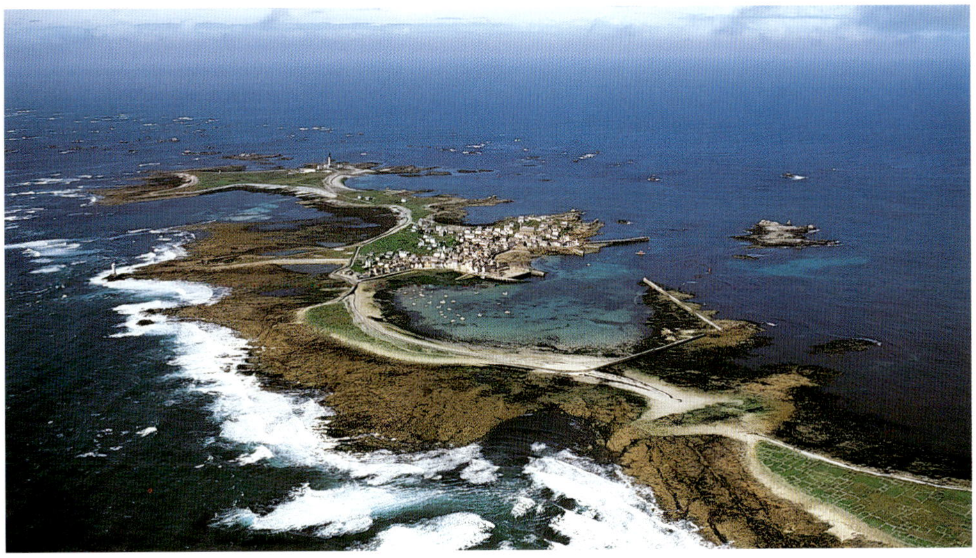

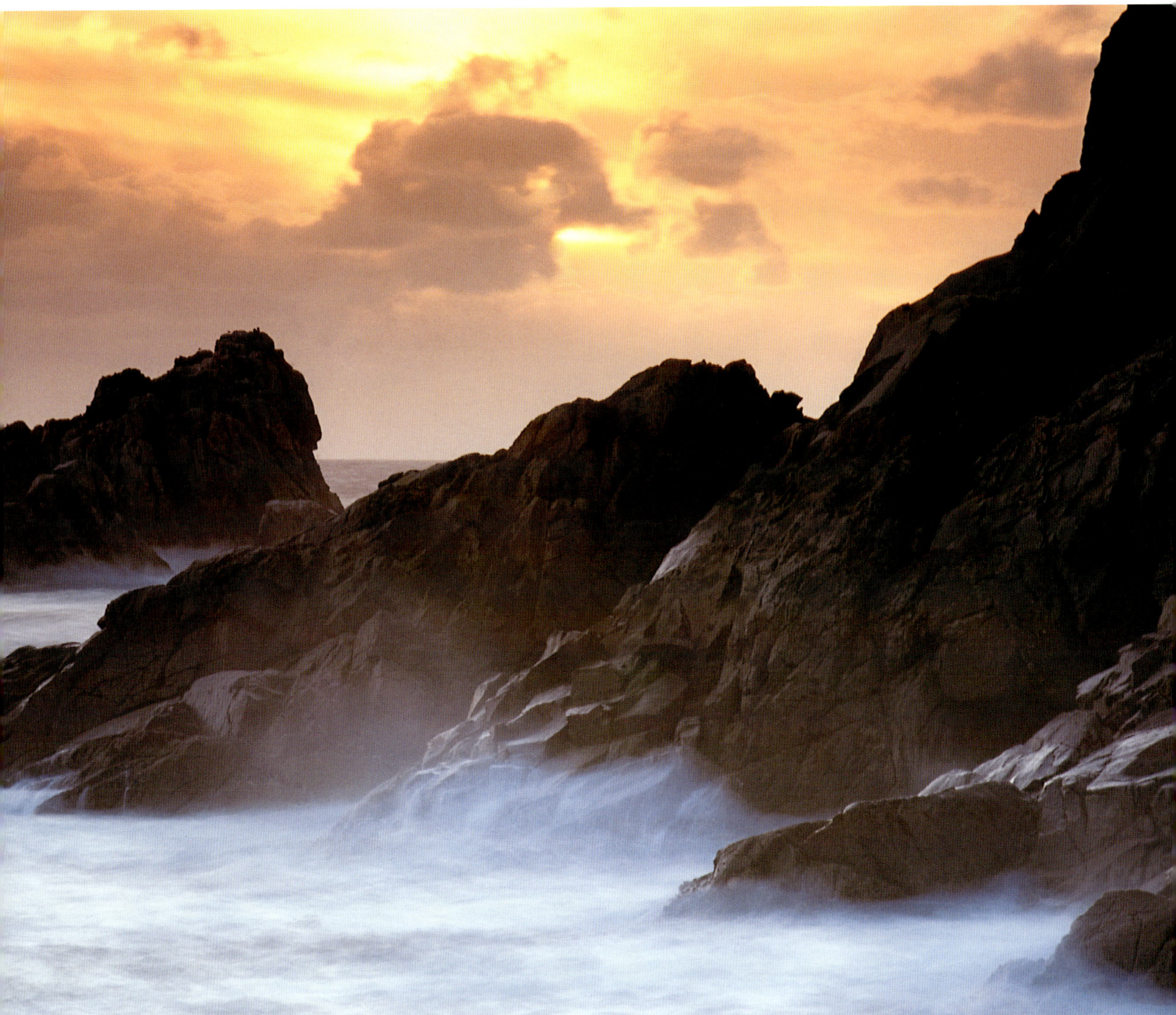

80 bottom This pair of farmers is cutting the hay that will serve as food for the animals during the winter. This practice is quite rare now because cows and horses, which numbered respectively 600 and 400 at the beginning of the 20th century, have nearly disappeared from the island, which has progressively been converted to tourism.

80-81 With a surface area of 3830 acres (1550 hectares), the ancient Uxisama is one of the largest — and most distant — islands of Brittany. Life there is difficult for the locals. Of the 3,000 inhabitants on the island prior to the First World War, a little over 800 remain. Numerous homes are shuttered up at the end of summer.

80 top The rams of Ouessant are small, with black heads and paws. They had disappeared from the island and would have become extinct without the perseverance of breeders from the region of Vannes. The islanders, for their part, preferred to raise larger rams from the continent, ones that can graze freely on the island from September to February. Each year the breeders bring their animals to the famous fair that, according to tradition, takes place the first Wednesday of February.

81 top At Ouessant the landscape is flat and barren. No trees, few slopes, only a carpet of heather and broom as far as the eye can see. Until recently — the beginning of the 20th century — the islanders dried cow and horse dung to use as fuel.

82 bottom Housed since 1961 in the ancient arsenal of Rue Vauban, the Fishing Museum attractively presents the evolution of this activity from its origins to the most modern techniques (tuna-fishing nets, whalers, techniques and equipment for fishing for cod, sardines, etc.).

82-83 A multitude of sailboats populates the port of Concarneau. Behind them a modern fishing boat reveals the true nature of the center of Cornouaille where sea-faring activity involves a large part of the local population and constitutes the principal economic resource.

83 top left Though the ancient sailboats for tuna fishing have disappeared from the ports of Groix and Belle-Île, their motorized offspring have an important position in the Concarneau fishing industry. Since the 1960s, Concarneau has been the leading port for deep-sea tuna fishing.

83 top right Scampi, enjoyed with black bread and homemade mayonnaise, are a delight. At night, the fishing boats leave the ports of Léchiagat, Guilvinee and Loctudy to catch this tasty prey in the wide basin in which they live, a few miles off the coast of Cornouaille.

82 top Concarneau is not only an important historical site hidden behind the bastions of its city walls, it is also a pleasant tourist port located near the Glénans Islands, a few miles from the small island of Groix.

The south? The south is all in its port towns, large and small, where many people today still live from the generous depths of the sea. Guilvinec and its lobster catchers who leave early in the morning to search in the "large basin." And Concarneau, famed for its maritime museum situated within the city walls and for its fishing boats that leave for tuna-fishing expeditions off the western coast of Africa. And that myriad of sheltered harbors, lit by the first rays of spring sunlight, blossom in a riot of lively colors! Names that are poetry: Merrien, Brigneau, Rosbras, where learning to sail and be initiated in the rudiments of navigation is wonderful. Doëlan, with its pink house that acts as a beacon when you arrive from the Island of Groix, and its Captain Cook cannery, one of the last examples of an industry that gave work to thousands of people, especially women, from Douarnenez to Belle-Île en Mer. Going up the Aven starting from Rosbras, you arrive in the small village of Pont Aven. This is where Paul Gauguin set down his backpack, brushes and easels between 1886 and 1888, inviting his friends and students to stay, from Paul Sérusier to Emile Bernard. All of them were attracted by the rough, authentic coast of a Brittany which, in their eyes, was in no way inferior to the mystification caused by Polynesia. It was this corner of Cornwall that inspired masterworks such as *La belle Angèle*, who not finding herself so beautiful at least in this depiction, categorically rejected the painting. This period also produced *Le Christ jaune* (The Yellow Christ), *Les ramasseuses de varech* (The Seaweed Gatherers), and *Les petites Bretonnes au bord de la mer* (Little Breton girls on the Seashore). Still echoing at Pont Aven are the interminable discussions of Xavier Grall, the most productive Breton poet writing in the French language of the 20th century who, at Nicole Corelleau's bar, with his friends Georges Perros and Glenmor, reorganized the world, Brittany, in particular, which he dreamed would be free and clear of the burden of dishonor.

83

84 top Rue de Kereon, with its rush-mat buildings that escaped the disastrous fire of 1762, is one of the most crowded streets of the old Quimper. It represents the obligatory and picturesque passage of the Défilé des Guises, which, during the last week of July, concludes the famous Festival of Cornouaille.

84 bottom The Odet, Quimper's river, which rises in the Black Mountains, is an enchanting stream of water, crossed over by numerous little bridges decorated with splendid geraniums.

84-85 Place Laennec is one of the most beautiful squares of Quimper. During the traditional festivals of Cornouaille, when bagpipers and talabarders blow with full lungs on these characteristic instruments, the city reaches the peak of its fascination.

On the opposite shore of the Laïta, to the west of which rises the charming town of Quimperlé, there is Lorient, the ancient Orient, created by Louis XIV to receive the ships of the East India Company, bringing into question its military "vocation" as it was gradually affirming its Celtic identity. Was it not in this great fishing port, in particular, in arsenal buildings converted to civilian use, or de-militarized, that Breizh TV, the "television of the sea, of Brittany, of the Celtic land," received its baptism in September 2000? Can anyone imagine a better symbol, a more stirring program, a change over more sensational and significant? It should be said that the city, which has hosted an Interceltic Festival competently directed by Captain Pichard since 1971, is the Mecca of a Celtic identity which has now liberated itself of complexes, both of superiority and inferiority.

85 top left It is pleasant to walk in Quimper's historical centre, freed from the bonds of traffic, wrapped in the perfume of kouign (a typical sweet of flour, eggs and sugar), crêpes and small focaccia.

85 top right At rue Kereon 9, this maiden of multicoloured wood wears the glazic costume of Quimper. Until the middle of the 20th century, many dressed in the traditional clothing of the city.

85

86 top The southern coast of Belle-Île, swept by storms, is a world of high cliffs and steep promontories. The stacks of Port-Coton had the honour of being painted by Monet, who stayed on the island in 1886.

86 center At Belle-Île, the bridge to the closed door of the city built in 1549 and later enlarged and modified by Vauban. It fell into the hands of the English who occupied it between 1761 and 1763. Now private property, it houses an interesting museum devoted to the history of the island and some of its celebrated visitors.

86 bottom Flowering meadows, tamarisk bushes, white walls, red raspberries and blue skies characterize southern Brittany.

86-87 Under the summer sky, the harbour of Sauzon, which numbers 703 inhabitants, on the northern coast of Belle-Île, takes on a vaguely Mediterranean aspect.

87 top Groix, a short distance from the city of Lorient, presents itself as a huge vessel of stone with the prow turned toward the west. The island gave birth to the sweet poet of the Breton language, Yann-Ber Calloc'hn whose most famous verses Me zo ganet e kreizh ar more were set to music by Jeff Le Penven and masterfully interpreted by Alan Stivell.

Facing the great Atlantic port is the Île de Groix which, just like Belle-Île, its neighbor farther to the south, nostalgically recalls the glorious days of prodigious tuna fishing and the canning industry. In the days of the merchant marines, it employed a fairly numerous workforce since its position in the open sea gave it an advantage over Lorient. Here, curiously, on the village tower, it is not a rooster that signals the direction of the wind but, in memory of an opulent past, an albacore tuna!

It is certainly an island of fishermen but also of farmers. It is an island sacrificed to mass tourism (although to a lesser degree than its neighbor) because of its magnificent panoramas, its vertiginous cliffs on the southern coast and its convex Grand Sables beach, starred with fragments of granite. But it is also an island of poets and bards. Yann Ber Calloc'h, the author of *Ar en deulin* (Kneeling), one of the most sensitive poets in the Breton language, was born here. Killed in the trenches in 1917, he left us the marvelous *Me zo ganet e kreizh ar mor* (I was born in the middle of the sea), set to music by the composer Jeff Le Penven and masterfully interpreted by Alan Stivell. Then there is Gilles Servat, who began playing the guitar here at the beginning of the 1970s. Gilles Servat? The bard, originally from Nantes, conveniently established himself a short distance from here near Etel, a place in which you don't know where the water ends and the earth begins. And that must have been precisely what Polo, Gilles' dog, thought the last time we went there to take photos at the very end of the Locoal harbor, lost between the "path of the Chouans" and the "distaff of Saint Brigate," when, slipping on a clump of seaweed, he found himself in the water!

Here you enter into the world of rebels, rebels with big hearts, the world of those who, when the time is right, can rise up against any form of tyranny and oppression.

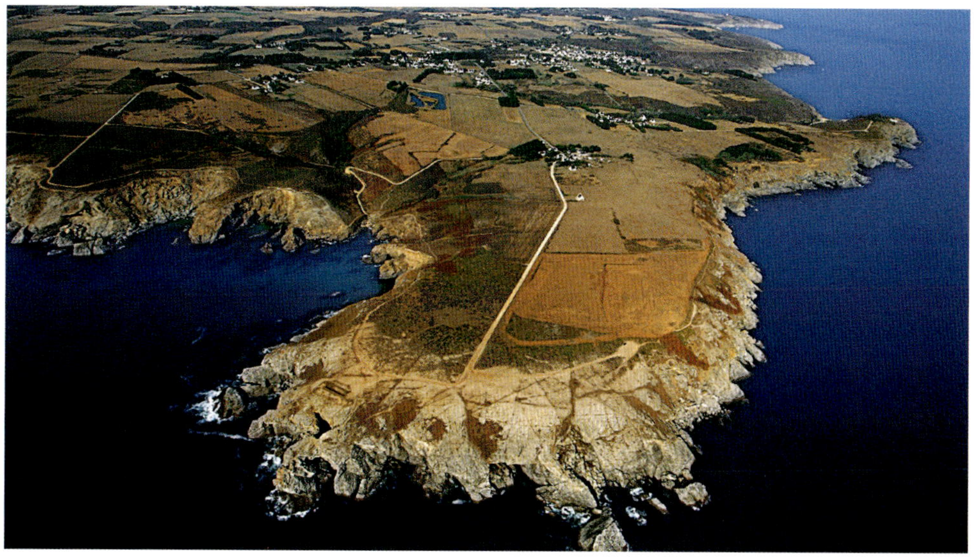

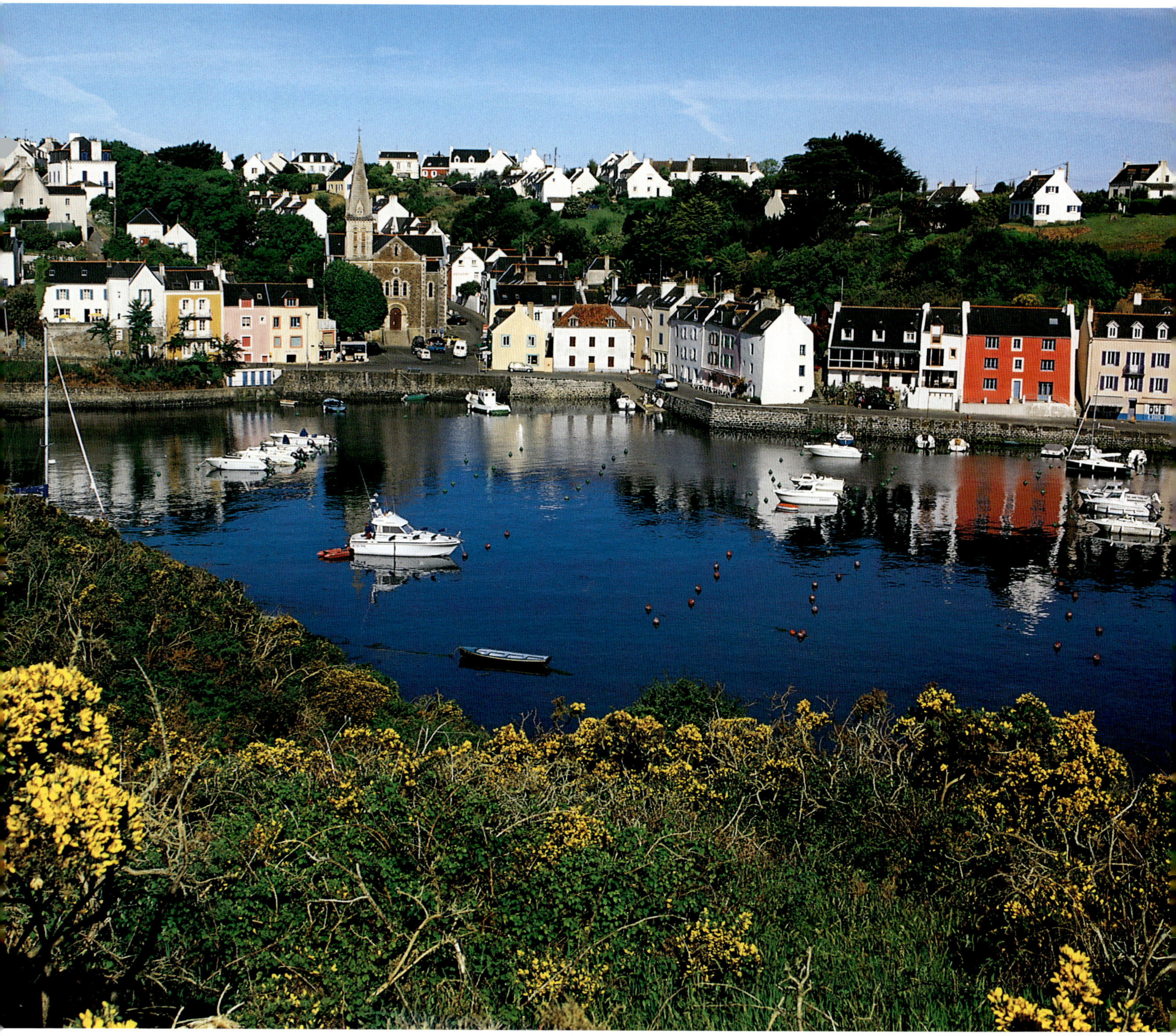

88 top Straw roofs are a traditional element of Breton architecture. Beginning at the end of the 19th century, following decrees and incentives, slate replaced straw and rush in the coverings. But in the region of Vannetais and in lower Cornouaille, this type of building survives even today, as in the village of Poul Fetan en Quistinic shown here.

88-89 Carnac is the richest megalithic site in Europe. The configuration of Menec, Kerlescan and Kermario can count a good 3,000 menhir, a Breton term that specifically means "long stone." Local legend would have it that you can recognise some Roman soldiers petrified by Saint Cornély, a Christian transposition of the god Cernunos.

89 top left The placement of these megaliths and the arrival of the Celts are as far away in time as the defeat of the Vénètes and the computer civilisation! So the appealing Obelix with his menhir on his shoulders is a pleasing anachronism!

89 top right The large menhir of Locmariaquer, broken into five parts, was one of the tallest in Brittany.

88 bottom The Suscinio castle on the Rhuys peninsula, a few steps away from the Atlantic Ocean, is one of the most beautiful forts in Brittany. Built in the 13th century, this residence, preferred by the dukes of Brittany, was altered in the 14th and 15th centuries. It is now the property of the Conseil Général du Morbihan, which has beautifully restored it.

Pressing ahead to the east, you arrive in the territory of the proud Vénètes. At the end of the summer in 56 B.C., in a bloody naval battle off the shores of the Rhuys peninsula, they were defeated by Caesar's ships under the command of Brutus. Their capital was in Locmariaquer, where you find the Merchants' Table, which even now gives rise to controversies and imagination, and the broken menhir, which, before being damaged, was undoubtedly the most important in France or perhaps, after all, the Gulf of Morbihan, which, it is said, includes as many islands as there are days in a year.

In any case, the region is the richest in Brittany with, to the west of Carnac, its covered walkways, its tumuli and its extraordinary alignments if Kermario, Menec and Kerlascan, vestiges, according to the most recent archaeological studies, of ancient astronomic "temples" and, to the east, on the Rhuys peninsula, the castle of Suscinio, superbly restored by the Morbihan General Council.

89

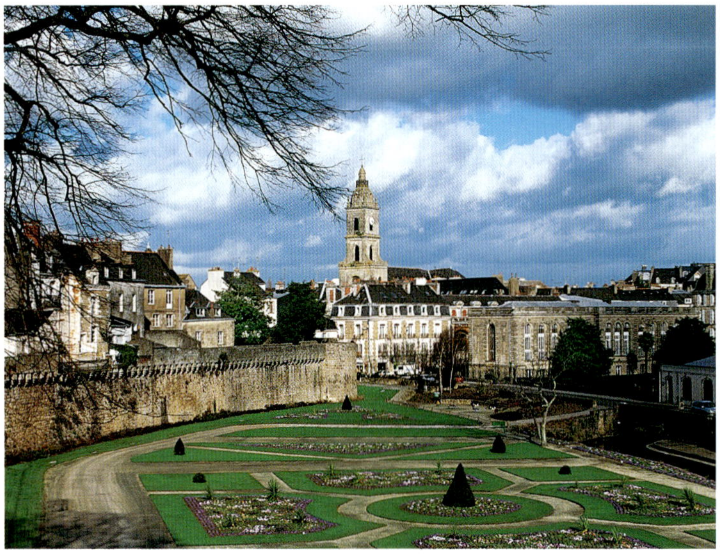
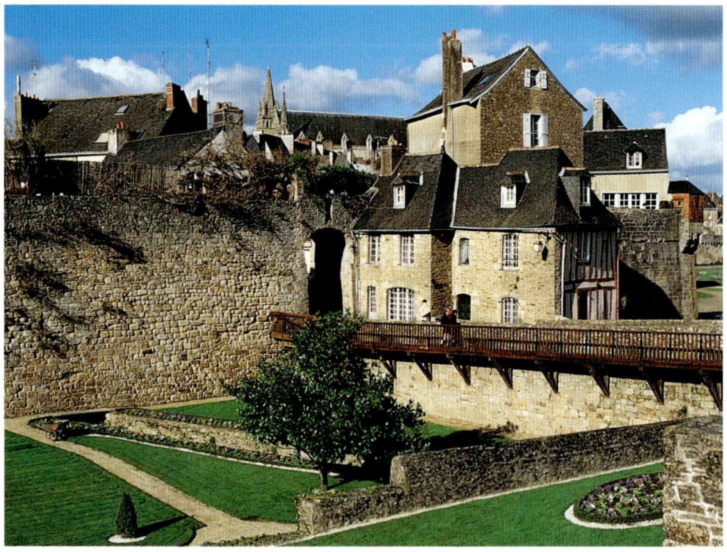
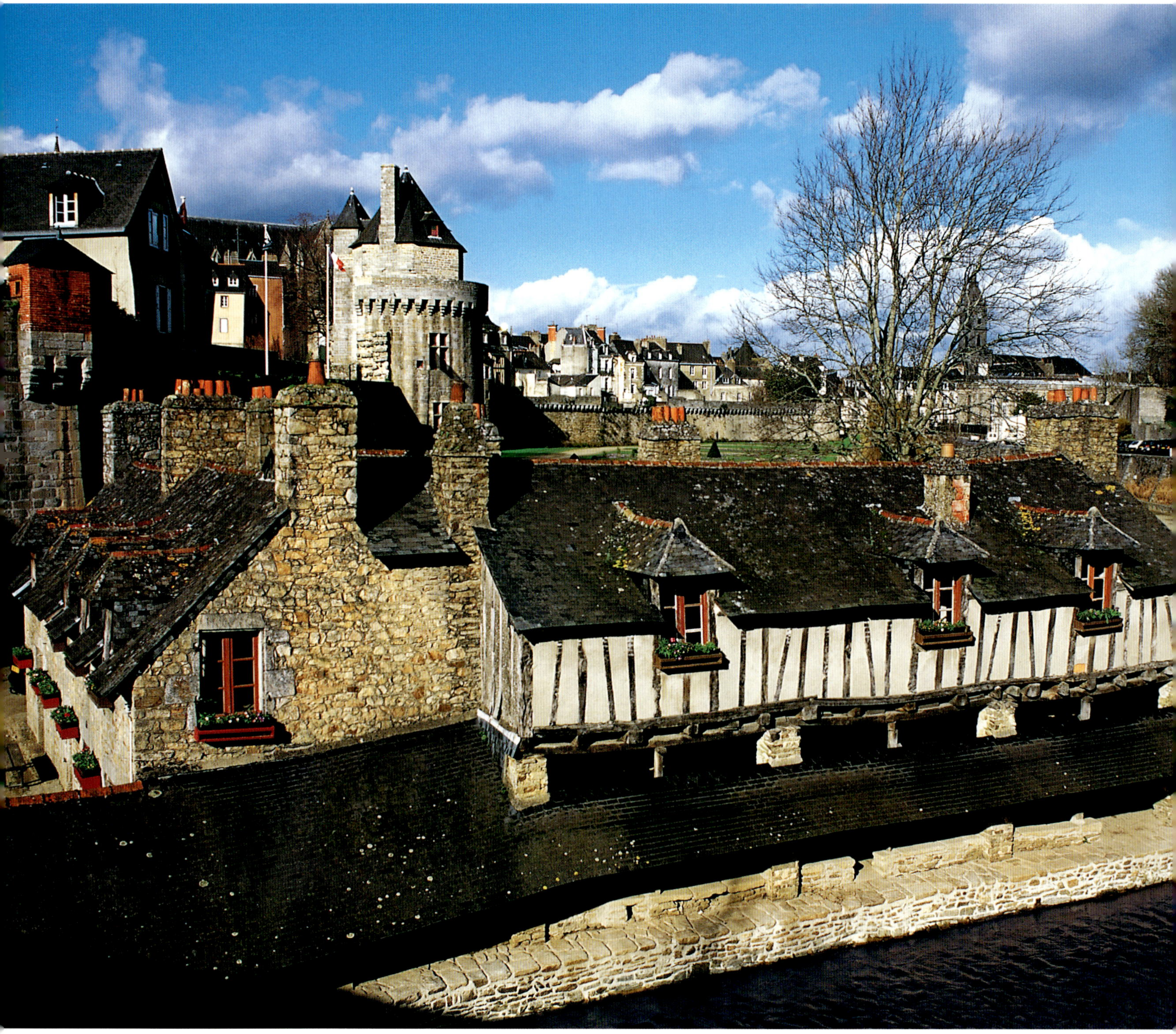

90 top left The splendid park of the ancient ducal palace of Vannes, open to the public since the 17th century, is a traditional destination for pleasant, relaxing walks in the heart of a dynamic city that numbers 52,000 inhabitants.

90 top right Vannes, the ancient Dariorutum, took its current name, that of the city of the Vénètes, around the 3rd or 4th century A.D. Its 13th-century walls were in part built along the perimeter — and the ruins — of the Gallic-Roman walls.

90-91 The old washing troughs along the Marle, with the bastions and the Tour du Connétable behind, offer a picturesque view of ancient Vannes that inspired several painters. They date from the beginning of the 19th century.

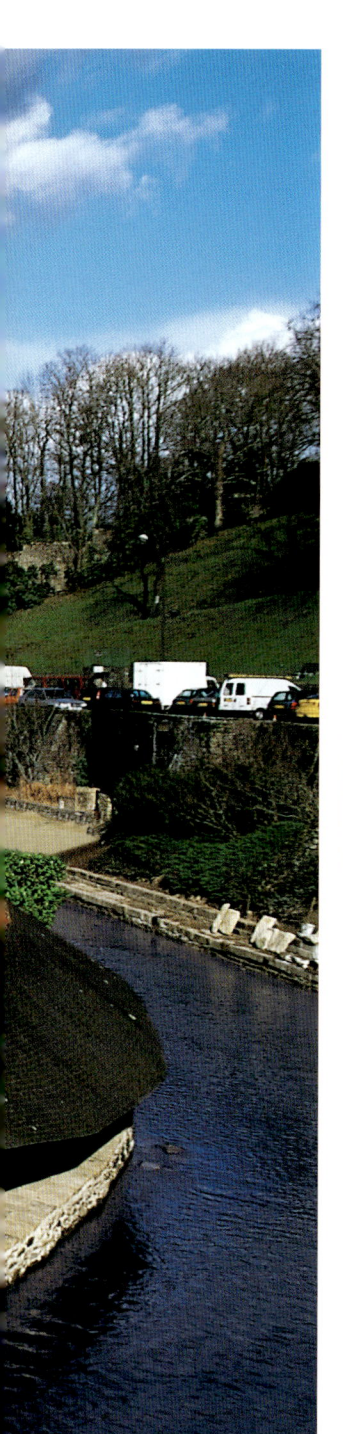

Vannes was the city of Nominoé, the first King of Brittany, in the 9th century. Later, in the Middle Ages, it became the residence of the Dukes of Brittany and then, after annexation to France and the revolt of the Red Berets, the seat of the Breton Parliament. Within its walls, some parts of which go back to the Gallic-Roman era, this lovely city still preserves an astonishing series of 16th-century rush-mat buildings in Rue Noë and Rue Saint-Samson.

91 left The Hermine Castle, not far from the Saint Vincent gate, is adjacent to the sumptuous French-style gardens of the ancient capital of the Bro Warok.

91 top right The inhabitants of Vannes, nestled at the end of the Gulf of Morbihan, inherited from the Vénètes' maritime power a special attraction for the sea. In the tourist port, *freed in the 1970s from the mud that obstructed it, boats of synthetic materials replaced heavy oak vessels, but the passion for sea-going adventures remains the same.*

91 bottom right The center of Vannes, near Henry IV square, rue des Halles and rue Saint-Salomon, teems with rush-mat houses from the 16th century.

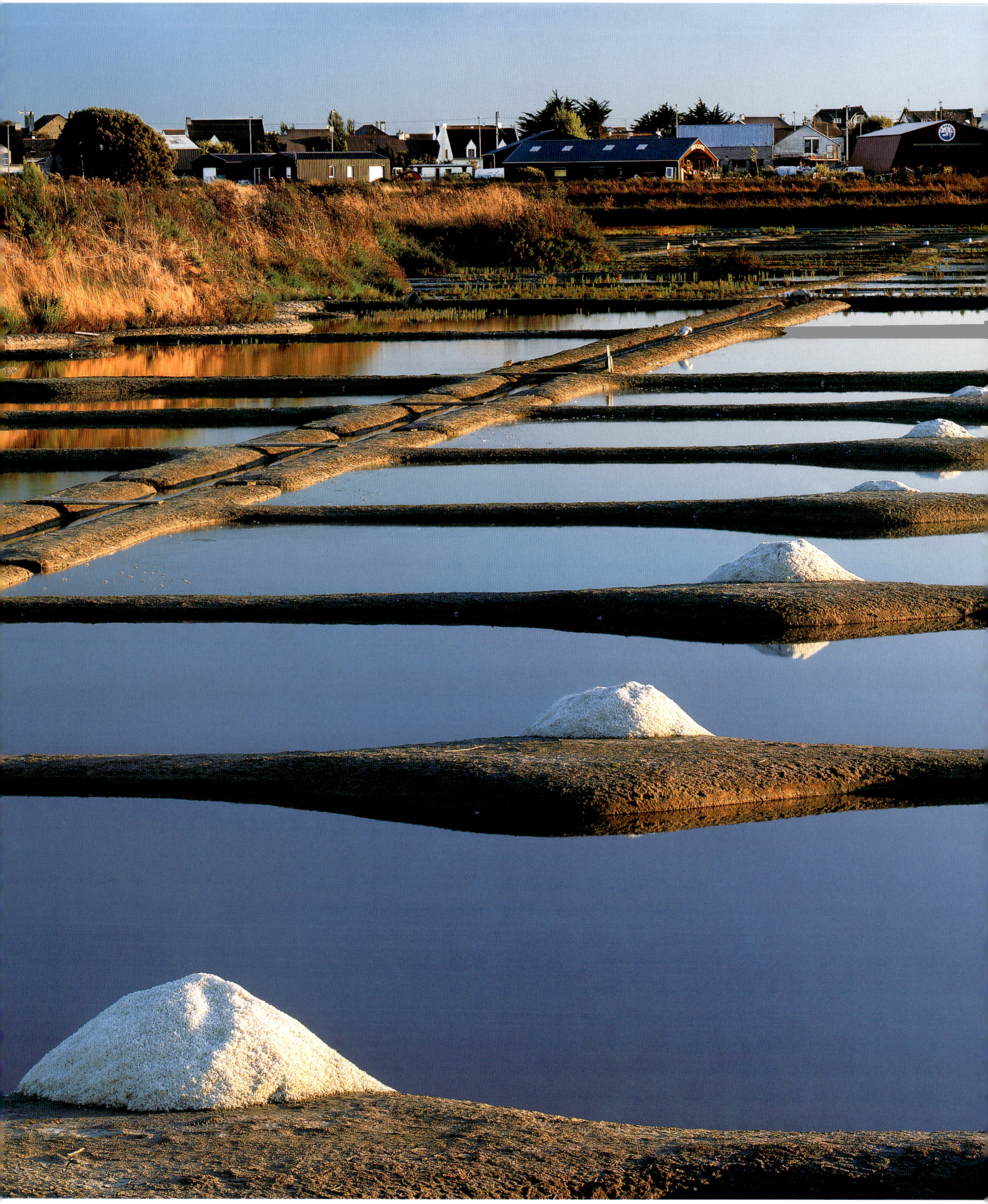

93 top Blain Castle, construction of which began in 1104, was the property of Olivier de Clisson before passing to the Rohan family, The façade, called the "residence of the king" (15th century) has preserved the fascination of the Breton Renaissance architecture.

93 center This photograph combines evidence of two past eras: the windmill, which recalls to mind Gilles Servat's beautiful song "turn, turn wings of the Guérande windmill" and a megalithic tomb from approximately 4,000 B.C.

93 bottom La Brière is marshy area of about 20,000 acres (8,000 hectares) which is part of a regional park created in 1970. In 1461 the inhabitants of the region were recognised by François II, duke of Brittany, a right of undivided property respected up till our times.

A panorama of Armorica, this coastal stretch some 6 miles (10 km) long that forms the contours of Brittany, would be incomplete without the Pays Nantais which, after the Revolution, made up the Department Loire-Atlantique. In a 1941 decree it arbitrarily separated from the administrative region of Brittany, in total disregard of the wishes of the overwhelming majority of the population.

And thus it was that, at Batz-sur-Mer, in that brackish lagoon that had represented the wealth of the area from the Middle Ages on, Breton was spoken until World, War I. And wasn't the splendid city of Guérande, the Breton Gwenrann, fortified by Duke Jean IV to defend himself from the terrible war of succession that saw the Breton party of Monfort opposed to that of the francophile Penthiève?

92-93 Around the village of Batz, where Breton has been spoken since World War I, the salt marshes are a silent, mineral world. The mirrors of salt water represented the wealth of the Guérandese peninsula in the period when Brittany was exempt from taxes on salt. This "privilege" was inexorably suppressed after the famous night of August 4, 1789.

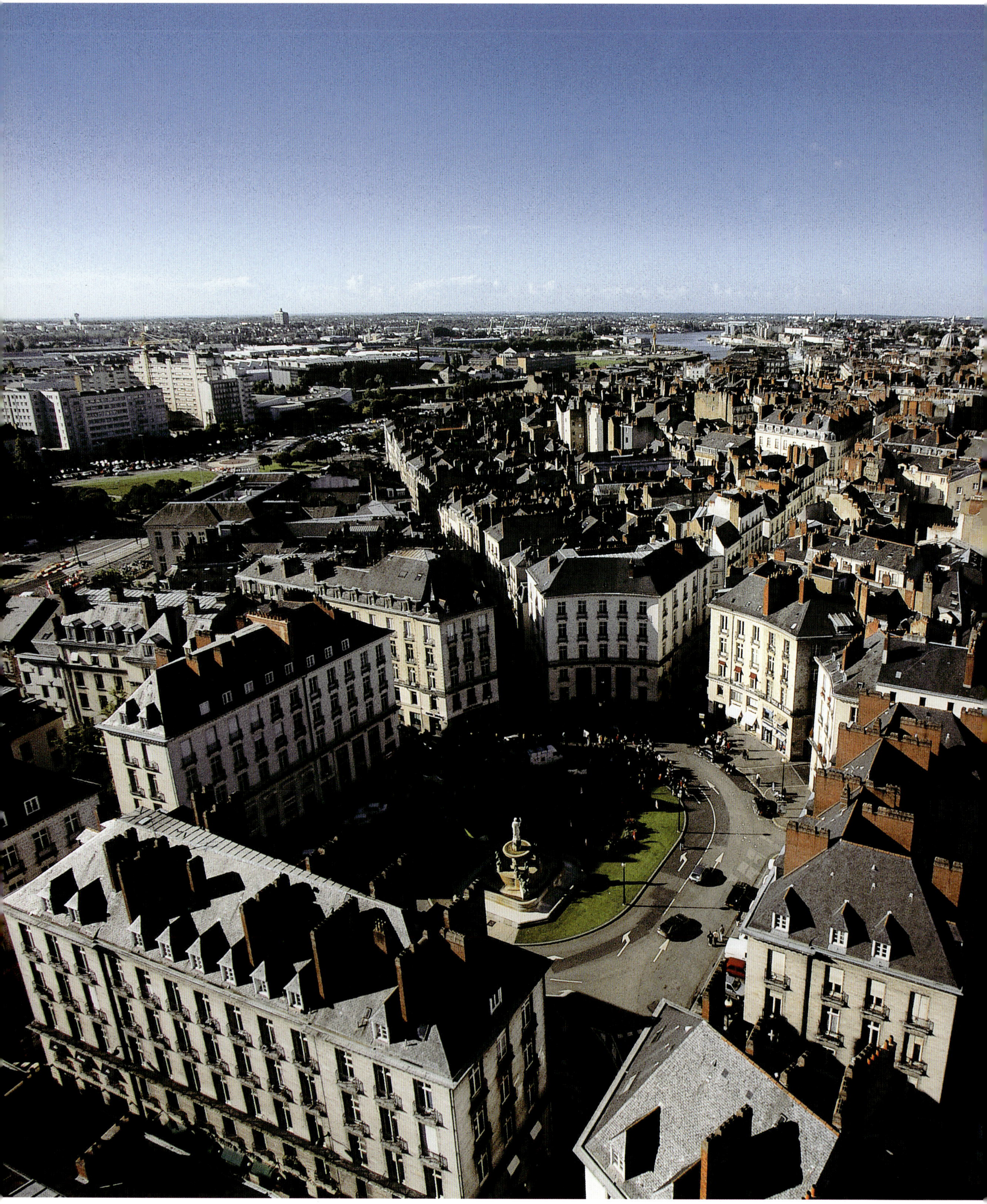

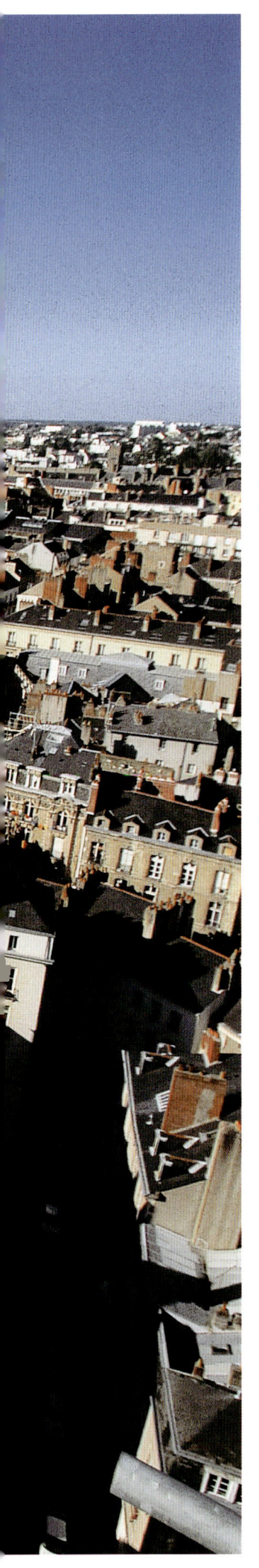

94-95 The Graslin di Nantes quarter came into being between 1778 and 1788. Place Royal, with its beautiful fountain, is the symbol of this section of the city, martyred by the bombardments of September 16 and 23, 1943.

95 The Loire (Liger in the Breton language) is one of the most beautiful rivers in France. Before being covered, the numerous branches in which it spread out made the historic capital of Brittany a true Venice of western Europe.

Though the seaside resort of La Baule, the vacation spot for the golden youth of France and Navarre, should be mentioned for having the most beautiful, longest beach in Europe, attentive travelers will indulge with pleasure in Nantes which, in 937, was chosen as the capital by Duke Alain Barbe-Torte, who had defeated the Normans.

In the city, there is still the ducal castle built at the end of the sixteenth century by François II and his daughter Anne, the last sovereign of the country. Following an unjust war, she was constrained to marry the King of France, Charles VIII. The tomb of François II and his wife, Margherite de Foix, sculpted in 1502 by Michel Colombe, is now found in the Cathedral of Saint Pierre while the shrine containing Anne's heart, profaned during the Revolution, can be seen at the Musée Dobrée.

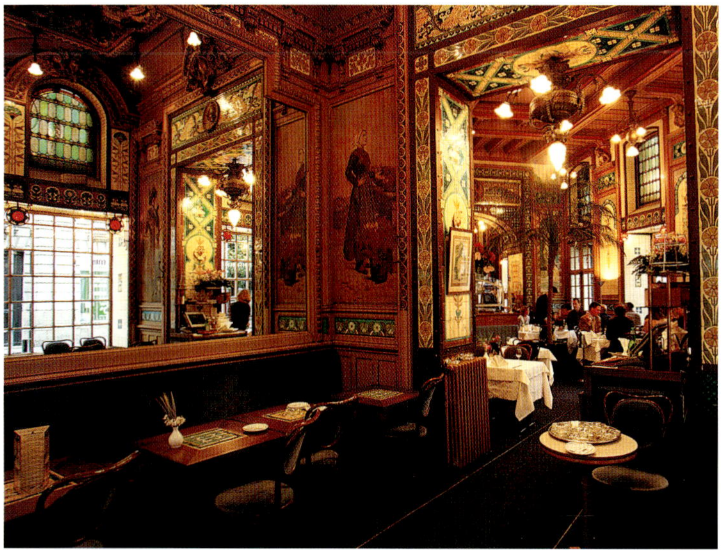

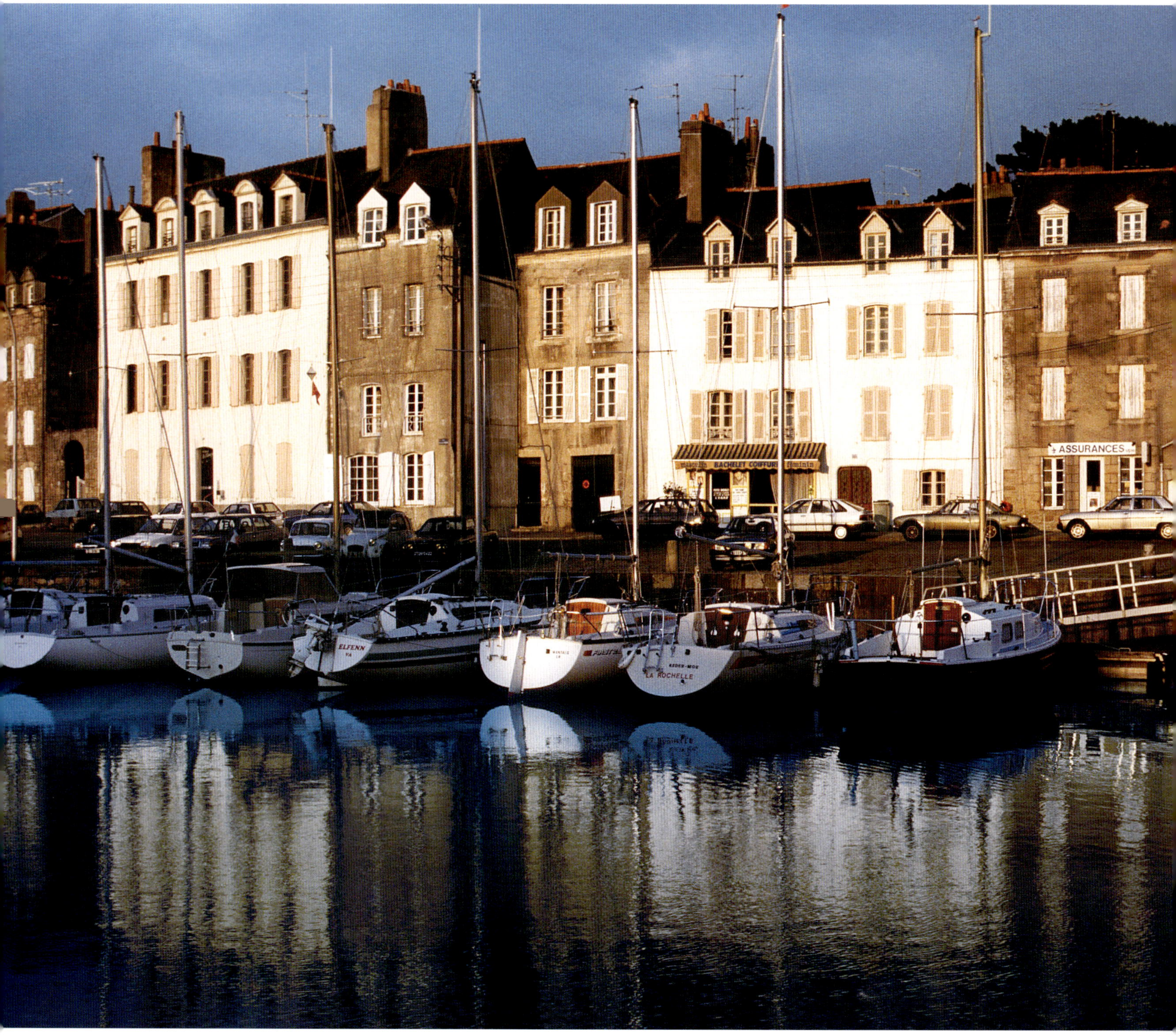
ASSURANCES
ELFENN
LA ROCHELLE

96 top Declared a historic monument, this 1900 brasserie with ceramic decorations on Place Graslin is an peerless temple to the gastronomy of Nantes.

96-97 Nantes is a port city about 50 miles (80 km) from the sea. It was this that made the city's fortune, in particular with the so-called "triangular trade," an elegant euphemism for the sale of slaves. Now the boats calmly moored at the docks wait to sail off on less immoral cruises.

97 top left The Pommeraye tunnel is a true myth for Nantes. Completed in 1843, it joins rue de la Fosse and the stock market located in rue Santeuil. The structure is divided into three levels, which are joined by a staircase made of iron and wood.

97 bottom left Within the Castle of the Dukes of Brittany are preserved the remains of the old Musée des Salorges, devoted to the history of the industrial and commercial activity of the city.

97 top and bottom right Created in 1880, the Musée des Beaux Arts is housed in a 19th-century building. The museum can boast of a notable collection of works by great masters, among them The Denial of Saint Peter by Georges de La Tour; the prized Madame de Senonnes, by Jean-Auguste Ingre; Caïd, Moroccan Captain by Eugène Delacroix; and Gathering Apples by Emile Bonnard.

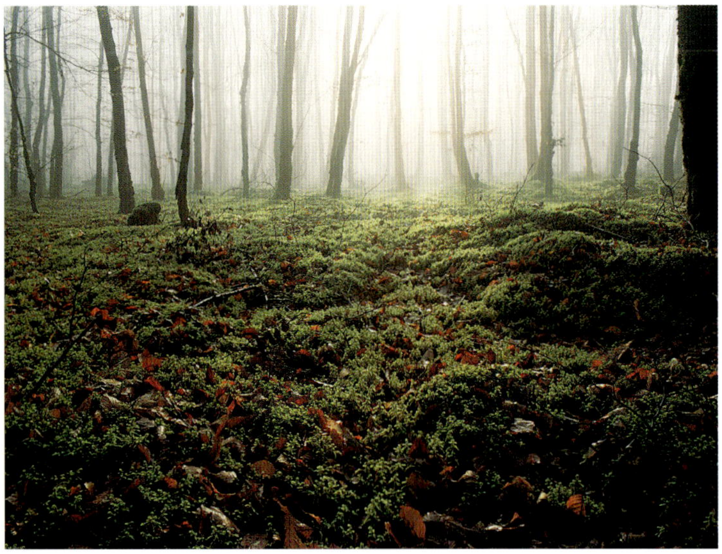

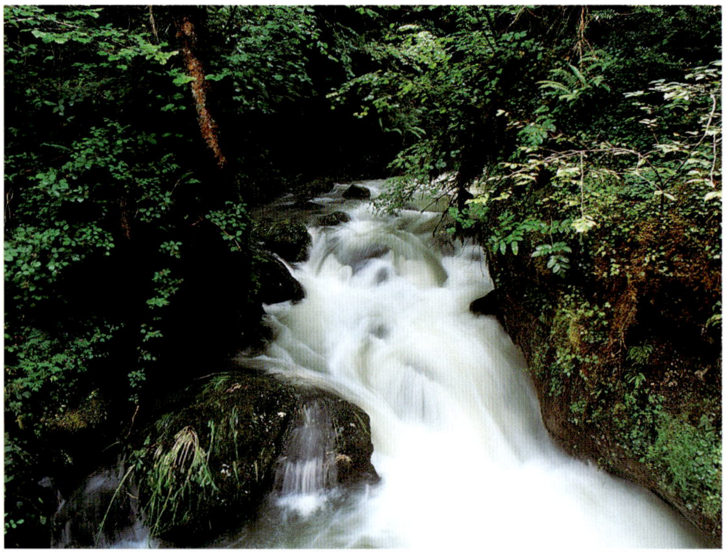

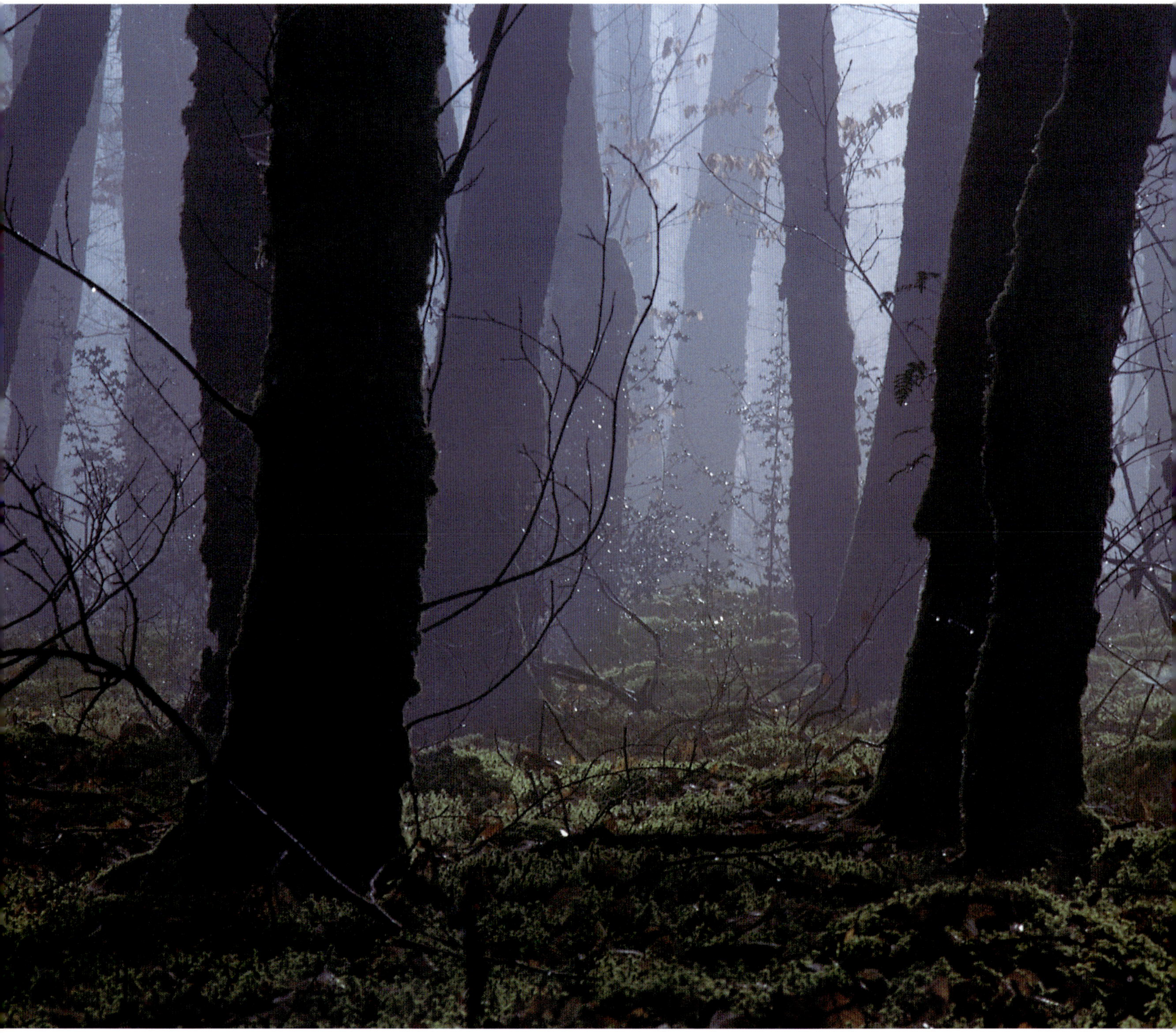

ARGOAT: THE 'LAND OF WOODS'

98 top left The "des Forges" pond, in the forest of Brocéliande, recalls the days when the area was mined for its abundance of iron, which gives the earth and the watercourses their characteristic color.

98 top right Whether pond, river or stream, water in all its forms is omnipresent in the forest of Merlin and Arthur and creates a perfect setting in which to let the imagination run free.

98-99 Dawn on a winter's day in the forest of Brocéliande. To the Celts the forest is the sacred universe par excellence, *and is inhabited by the creatures of the Other World.*

99 bottom The enchanting path of Sainte Barbe au Faouët, in the woods of Cornouaille, evokes the ghost of Marion "Finefont," or 'Marion of Faouët', the famous kilted leader of a band of 'fearless' brigands, who plundered the entire region in around the mid-18th century.

A*r mor,* the sea. *Ar goat,* the "land of woods" — a name which, like the narrow strip of coastline it refers to, echoes with the sounds of an unknown and mysterious world; a world of spirits, no doubt, of the *duz* Gauls and their countless descendents who in various degrees were loved, feared and respected. But it is also a world of outlaws, either terrible or extremely generous. Guy Eder de la Fontenelle, for example, who had nothing in common with Robin Hood and who terrorized the region in the days of the War of the Alliance, or Marion du Faouët ("of the beech tree"), who was hung in Saint Corentin Square, Kemper in 1755 after having cleaned out the Poher district at the head of a band of cutthroats. This is the world of the volunteers of Jean Cottereau, or Jean "Chouan," as he was known for his perfect imitation of the owl, and whose name became associated with the commoners' resistance against a Republic gone mad.

Ar goat! The land of woods that instil terror in those that do not know them and get lost in their depths, as in the case of the legionaries of Postumius in the dark forest of Litania. Yet it is also a hospitable land, a refuge that nurtures materially and spiritually those who for thousands of years have inhabited its forests, becoming part of them, merging with them, like the *korrigan,* the young fawn of the Afterlife, and all the small creatures of the night. The forest, in its association with *nemeton,* the sacred glade, is the heart of a wonderful world capable also of becoming an ally during conflicts, and not only for the sake of putting on an act a defense strategy. According to François Le Roux and Christian J. Guyonvarc'h, "the one true Celtic sanctuary is the dense, living forest which, at the dawn of history, covered immense stretches of Northern and Western Europe. Our Brocéliande is the last strip of that ancient treasure."

Brocéliande! Is this the forest that literally bewitched all the western courts when Geoffroy de Monmouth, Robert Wace, Robert de Boron and Chrétien de Troyes dared to narrate the adventures of the Knights of the Round Table, the madness of Merlin, the passions of Lancelot and Guinevere, the "white specter"? A multiform and multi-dimensional universe it is, which corresponds more to the geography of the soul than that of the land surveyors. Claudine Glot, President of the Centre de l'Imaginaire Arthurien (Centre of Arthurian Imagery) was not wrong when she said, "Brocéliande does not exist in administrative map-making. It is a forest that each one of us carries inside and each lives in the hope of finding."

100 top Built in reddish shale at the end of the 14th century by Jean de Trécesson, the castle that still bears his name today reflects somerly in the waters of the pond in front of it. This is undoubtedly one of the most fascinating parts of the forest of Brocéliande.

100 center The Tomb of Merlin, remains of an ancient covered passageway that was destroyed in the 19th century by a rather irreverent owner, is today the object of a zealous cult. Here hundreds of anonymous hands place votive offerings for the medieval personification of the great Cernunos.

100 bottom Comper Castle, in Brocéliande, houses the Centre for Arthurian Imagery. The most recent part of the building, dating back to 1860, is reserved for exhibitions and cultural events. The 15th-century ruins of the fortress overlook the moat.

Dame Claudine, who has come to identify herself so completely with the enchanted realm that some say she is a fairy, claims that "the Chart describing the habits and customs of Brocéliande Forest, which dates back to 1467, appropriately locates the realm of Merlin near Comper Castle" — exactly where Claudine set up the C.I.A. branch in 1990.

In the waters of the lake of Comper the love-struck Merlin built for his "pupil" Viviane a magnificent crystal palace, which merged with the lake itself, and where she taught Lancelot, making him the most courageous, skillful and beguiling knight of the Round Table.

In the Valley of No Return the terrible Morgana, part fairy, part witch, with the ambivalence typical of the creatures of the Afterlife, imprisoned her unfaithful lovers behind an invisible wall of air, until the handsome Lancelot, immunized by his ardent and pure love for Queen Guinevere, broke the spell forever.

A short distance away, to the northwest of Comper Castle, is the tomb of Merlin with the remains, more poignant than stunning, of a *hent korriganed*, literally "path of korrigan" or, less poetically, a covered passageway that was destroyed in the late 19th century.

Here votive notes are placed by thousands of anonymous hands, in a strange continuance (or revival?) of the worship of ancient figures.

100-101 According to legend and keen "Arthurians," in a palace hidden at the bottom of the Lake of Comper the fairy Viviane trained the handsome Lancelot, son of King Ban de Bénoïc.

101 top The stately splendor characterizing the buildings belonging to the castle of Trécesson, such as this circular dovecot, clearly illustrates the great wealth of the ancient local nobility.

102-103 Rochefort-en-Terre, a picturesque village of around 700 inhabitants, is situated right in the heart of Porhoët, a region characterised by shale and woodlands. Place du Puits, with its stone or wattled houses, many of which are enhanced with turrets and decorated with magnificent cascades of geraniums in bloom, presents a truly charming spectacle in Spring.

103 top left All that remains of the medieval castle of Rochefort-en-Terre, which was largely destroyed by Republican troops in 1793, is the small entrance building and some parts of the walls and outbuildings, restored in the early 20th century with elements from the manor house of Keralio, near Muzillac.

102 top Situated between forests and moorland, a few miles south of the Forest of Brocéliande in the direction of La-Gacilly, is the site known as Pierres Droites of Monteneuf, one of the finest megalithic sites in Brittany. More than forty of the 420 deep-red monoliths that originally stood on the site before they were pulled down in the late 10th century by militant Christians have recently been raised again.

102 bottom Around 31 miles (50 km) south of Rennes on the road to Redon is the megalithic site of Saint-Juste, one of the richest in the Argoat region. The western dolmen of Croix Saint-Pierre, dating back to 2500 B.C., offers a fine example of corridor burial.

Here is where Porhoët begins, whose original name *pou-tre-coët* is frequently translated as "Transylvania," although it simply means "wood-covered land."

Not far from Guer the "standing stones" of Monteneuf, which Canon Mahé wrote about in 1825 in his valuable essay on the relics of Morbihan, were patiently put back in place by compassionate hands at the end of the last century, after having been pulled down by Christians with equal dedication at the beginning of the second millennium. Today, these stones form the impressive background for the Arthurian Week celebrations. Here, in the Summer of 1997, the extraordinary Roland Becker and his Breton National Orchestra performed a series of gavottes that were rousing enough to wake the dead.

A few miles south-east and not far from route D 873, on the Moors of Lanveaux, which stretch out their cloak of heath and broom from Rochefort en Terre to Locminé, is the site of Saint-Juste, proof (if any were needed) that Argoat is in no way inferior to Armor from the point of view of its cultural heritage. The mounds of Château du Bé, overlooked by a *cromlec'h*, the *cairn* of Croix Saint-Pierre, the splendid burial place of Tréal, the Demoiselles de Cojoux and the alignments of Moulin, represent some of the most important megalithic concentrations of Brittany. A short distance away towards the south, where the rivers Oust and Vilaine meet, stands Redon, a city steeped in ancient history. Here, in the year 832, Nominoë, the first king of Brittany, built a monastery for the obvious purpose of claiming this borderland as part of his kingdom. The monastery buildings, today occupied by St. Saveur College, include an abbey church which is considered one of the masterpieces of Romanesque architecture in Brittany. A free port in the 18th century, one of the characteristic features of the city is its charming riverside towpaths in granite. Today it is the heart of the region of Redon, and proud of its cultural and musical heritage. Every year, in late October, the lively Festival de la Bogue d'Or is held, during which the most beautiful voices of "Gallésie" can be heard.

Moving westward, we quickly come to Rochefort-en-Terre, a real pearl of a village nestled in a valley rich in woodlands and orchards. Although the only remains of the ancient settlement are the small castle, certain sections of the ramparts and the outbuildings of Rochefort Castle, the village boasts a number of magnificent 16th- and 17th-century houses with superb granite or wattled façades and many with turrets, which can be seen along Rue du Porche and in the squares of des Halles and du Puits.

103 top right The abbey of Saint-Saveur di Redon, founded in the 9th century by Konwoéon, a relative of King Nominoë, for many years had a great influence over northern Brittany.

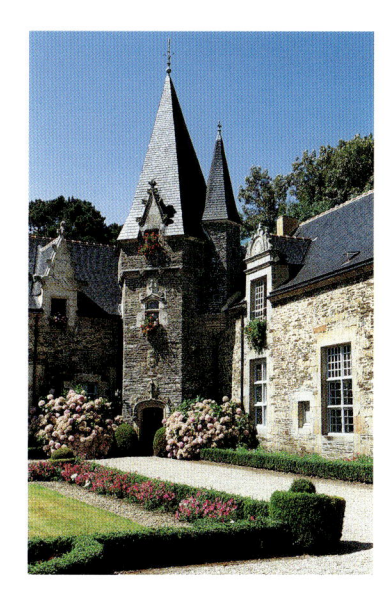

103

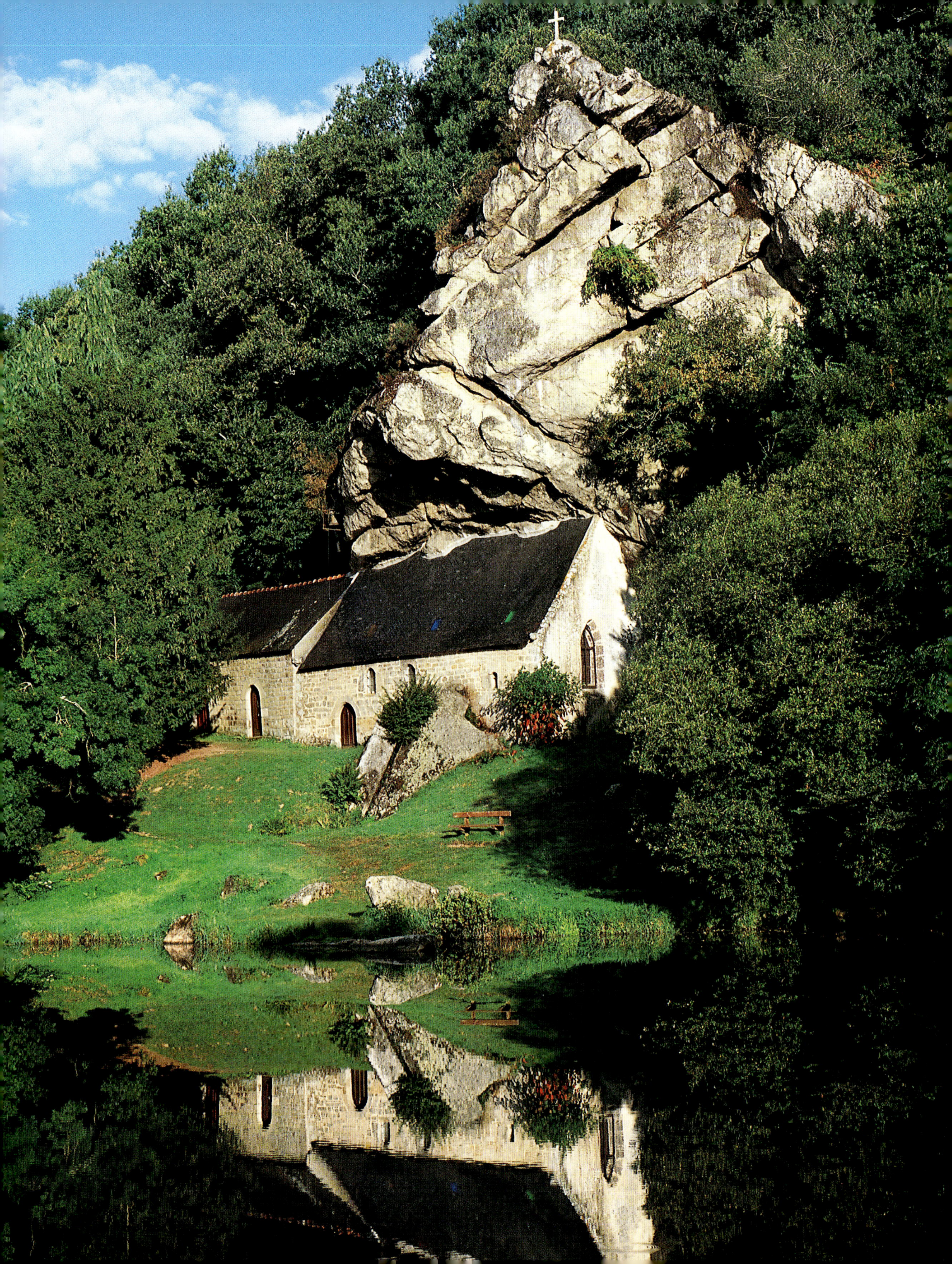

104 The Saint-Gildas hermitage, nestled in a peaceful loop of the River Blavet, is built into the rock.

105 top left The splendid castle of Largoët, better known by the name of 'Tours d'Elven,' is one of the most majestic of Brittany. The fortress, which was built by the lord of Rieux, a relative of Duke François II, was destroyed by the French troops of Charles VIII in 1488. All that remain are a fine 15th-century tower with skylight and an impressive octagonal-shaped keep which, with a height of 190 feet (57 m), is one of the tallest in Europe.

105 top right With its impressive structure the covered market of Questembert, dating back to 1552, is one of the oldest and finest of Brittany, along with that of Faoüet.

105 bottom The River Blavet, 122 miles (140 km) long, is ideal for those who choose to spend a quiet holiday in the countryside.

On the route from Rochefort to Vannes lies Questembert, once the setting for one of the most famous battles in the history of Brittany, which took place in the year 890 in a place named Coët-bihan, when King Alain le Grande, known as "Barbe-Torte," defeated the powerful Norman troops. On the site stands a small, obelisk-shaped monument bearing an inscription, both in French and Breton, commemorating the heroic king.

Before leaving the town, a visit to the covered market is a must. The market, which dates back to 1552, is composed of an extraordinarily harmonious structure with three arcades and is one of the last existing examples of its kind in Brittany.

At 9 miles (15 km) to the northeast, along the road from Vannes to Rennes, stands the castle of Largoët (or "the Towers of Elven," as it is still known today), which preserves within its huge stone walls the memory of one of the more unpleasant chapters in the history of Brittany. Owned by the Lord of Rieux, from 1472 to 1476 this castle was the prison of Henry Tudor, later King Henry VII of England, before Charles VIII's French troops burned it down in 1488. Today in ruins, the castle still manages to inspire awe in the visitor — the 11th-Century keep, for example, an impressive, six-story building, is almost 190 feet (57 m) high, making it one of the tallest in Europe.

In the town of Baud, which lies at the westernmost point of the woodland area stretching out across the Moors of Lanvaux, north of the Camors Forest, is one of the most mysterious statues of Brittany, known to the local people as the Venus of Qunipily. Visitors might well wonder how this little moss-covered granite figure, with its thighs like two stumpy tree-trunks and short, toad-like neck, could have come to be called Venus. Yet this stone "beauty" once stood proudly on the hill of Castennec, a few miles north, on the site where archaeologists believe the ancient Gallo-Roman *dunon* of Sulim stood, until it was torn down by zealous Christians in 1661 and hurled into the deepest part of the River Blavet. The statue remained underwater for three years until the local people, firmly attached to their idols and remote pagan rites and staunchly shrouded in superstition, recovered it and restored it to a place of worship. Subsequently, the "iron lady" was again thrown into the river by Reformists and again salvaged from the waters.

And there it would have remained if the local landlord, the Count of Lannion, had not decided — to his credit — to give it a home on his own property! Deprived of their idol, the villagers of Castennec were angered by this decision, but the 'Venus' finally found a place of rest. Roman deity, Egyptian Isis, or matron of the Cyclades, the goddess continues to keep secret her identity. The entire region, in actual fact, is steeped in mystery. A little north of Baud, for example, in the borough of Guénin, is Mane Gwenn ("white mountain" or "sacred mountain"), on which stands the chapel of St. Michel, probably built on the site of a temple dedicated to the god Bélénos. Dug into this extraordinary mass is a basin that continues to raise controversies and questions. Might it actually be a druidic sacrificial altar, as Gwenc'hlan Le Scouézec and Jean Markale believe?

106 The castle of Pontivy was built in the 15th century by Jean II of Rohan. Of the four original towers two remain, complete with trapdoors and corner turrets. Partly accessible to visitors, the castle houses interesting summer exhibitions dedicated to the history of Brittany.

106-107 Burnt down and pillaged during the Revolution, the Cistercian abbey of Bon-Repos, near the lake of Guerlédan and the forest of Quénéquan, was salvaged from the brambles thanks to the perseverance of a commendable group of individuals who dedicated their time and efforts to its recovery.

107 top left At Poul-Fetan, in the borough of Quistinic, this magnificent 16th-century village of huts was perfectly restored in the 1970s. The village faithfully reproduces the atmosphere of an ancient village of the Vannes region.

107 top right During the summer months in the town of Poul-Fetan a number of cultural associations organize a revival of various themes relating to the everyday life of the ancient inhabitants. Here, for example, we can see several young washerwomen in ancient dress wringing out the laundry by hand.

On the other side of the N24, which connects Rennes with the large port of Lorient, is the little settlement of Poul Fetan. Carefully and tastefully restored by the Council of Quistinic, this is one of the ancient little villages of huts that make Brittany so charming, especially around Bro Gwened (the region of Vannes). In the village, which dates back to the 16th century, are an ancient communal oven, a potter's workshop and an inn, which today serves a range of traditional Breton dishes. A local association raises several breeds of *pie-noire* cows, small-hooved but extremely tough animals that produce high-quality milk; during the 1970s the breed risked extinction, victim of the race for productivity. On the subject of the animal and plant life typical of Brittany, the association in charge of the village of Lann Gough in Melrand, a settlement similar to Poul Fetan, is currently working on the recovery of an extraordinary flora and fauna heritage, including the ditch goats, the so-called Ouessant rams and various other animal and plant species that were characteristic of Brittany in about A.D. 1000 — all within an exceptionally well-restored village of huts from the same period. A few miles north lies Bieuzy; here, built on the rock face in a loop of the River Blavet, opposite the site of Castennec where once stood the city of Sulim, is a magnificent chapel dedicated to Saint Gildas de Rhuys. Not far from the D2, on the winding road leading to Pontivy, is the 15th-century chapel of Quelven, which is famous mainly for the fact that it houses an extraordinary polychrome statue of St. George and the dragon, as well as for one of the rare opening Virgins of Brittany. During the August 15th processions (reminiscent of local pagan customs that the Church eventually adopted after failing to abolish them) an "angel" descends from the bell-tower of the parish church on a rope and proceeds to light a *tantad!* Towards the north-west, in the area of the Côte d'Armor, stands the Cistercian abbey of Bon-Repos (12th century), which was devastated and pillaged like many other religious monuments during the French Revolution. The picturesque ruins of the abbey are reflected in the emerald waters of Lake Guerlédan, a jewel nestling among the 6175 acres (2500 hectares) of beech and fir trees that make up the forest of Quénéquan. Ancient fief of the Rohan family, Pontivy has a magnificent fortified castle that today still boasts two large towers, complete with trapdoors and crowned with smaller watchtowers, which overlook the ancient town with its many 16th- and 17th-century buildings. Was it to cover up the fact that the Rohan family spent more time with the French royalty than with the dukes of Brittany, or that in the period of the Empire the bourgeois had renamed the town Napoléonville, that the independent movement set up a short-lived independent Breton government in July of 1940?

107

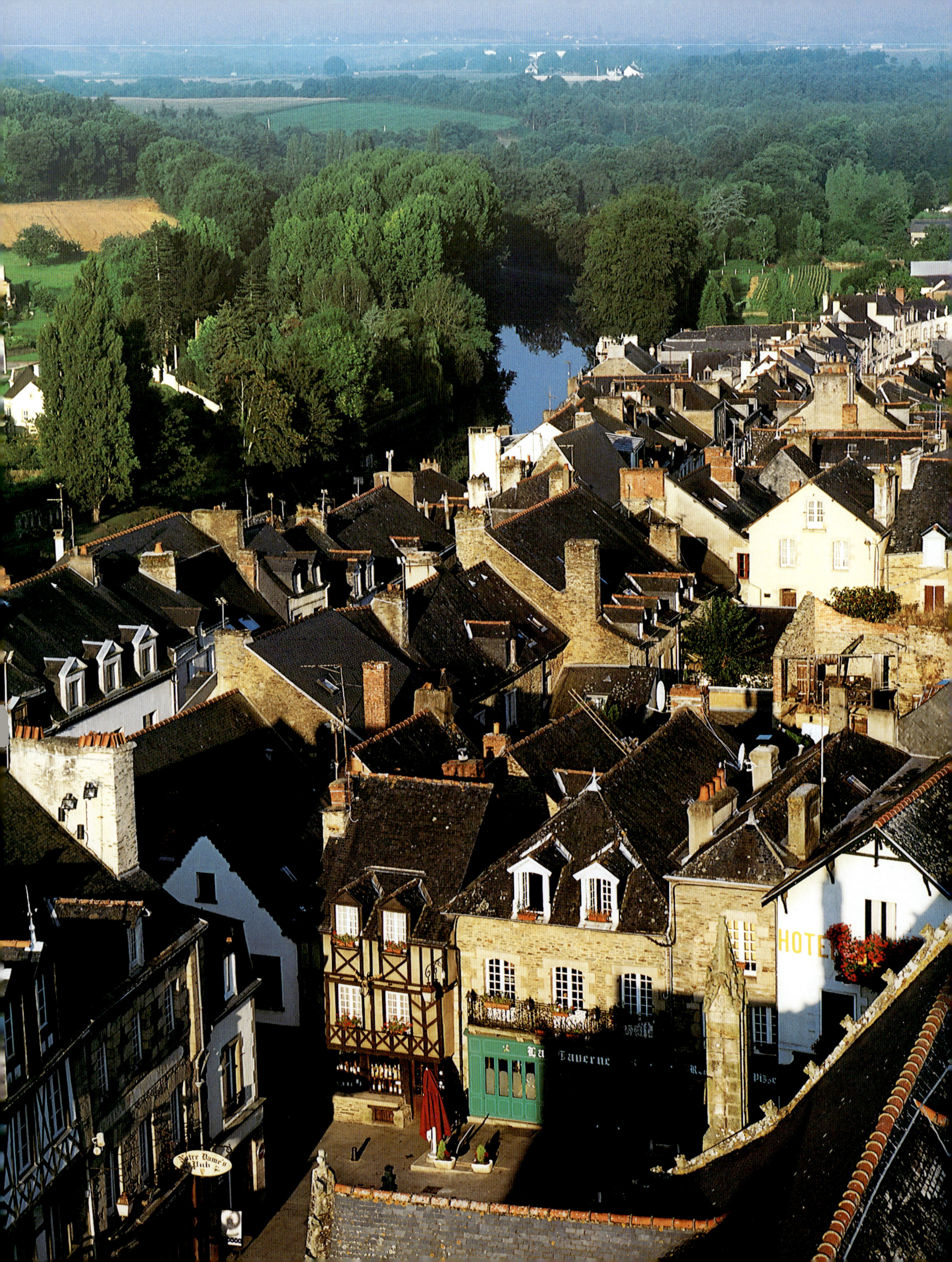
HOTE
Taverne

108 To the north of the moorlands of Lanvaux, in the heart of Porhoët, Josselin (the "village through the wood") is a charming, peaceful little town bounded by the River Oust.

108 top The Basilica of Notre-Dame du Roncier, in Josselin, houses the 15th-century mausoleum of Olivier de Clisson, who succeeded Bertrand du Guesclin as constable of France, and of his wife Marguerite de Rohan.

108 bottom The castle of Josselin, destroyed in 1488 by order of Duke François II as a punishment for the betrayal of Jean de Rohan, was rebuilt in the late 15th century. The stone interlacing of the central part of the castle contrasts strongly with the austere fortified structure of the interior façade.

Moving eastward, we come to Josselin, a delightful medieval town washed by the calm waters of the River Oust. This Breton town has the highest percentage of ancient wattled houses, of which that standing at no. 3, rue Georges Le Berd dates back to 1538. The castle, which has an internal façade covered with lace-like Gothic-flamboyant decorations, was first damaged by Duke François II, the father of Anne of Brittany, as a punishment to the owner, Jean de Rohan, guilty of offering his services to the King of France. Subsequently, at the beginning of the 17th century, Cardinal Richelieu had five of its nine towers destroyed. Nevertheless, the remains of the castle are truly magnificent, lending a touch of loftiness to the surrounding landscape. On the edge of the forest of Paimpont lies Ploërmel, which boasts some fine examples of 16th-century houses, especially in rue Beaumanoir, whose name recalls the heroic Combat des Trente, a battle fought at the height of the War of Succession of Brittany between thirty cavaliers of the pro-English faction and thirty paladins of the pro-French party. The church (on the porch of which the figure of a boar engaged in gustily playing the bagpipes clearly illustrates the ancient attitude of the clergy toward musicians) contains the tombs of dukes Jean II (1286-1305) and Jean III (1312-1341).

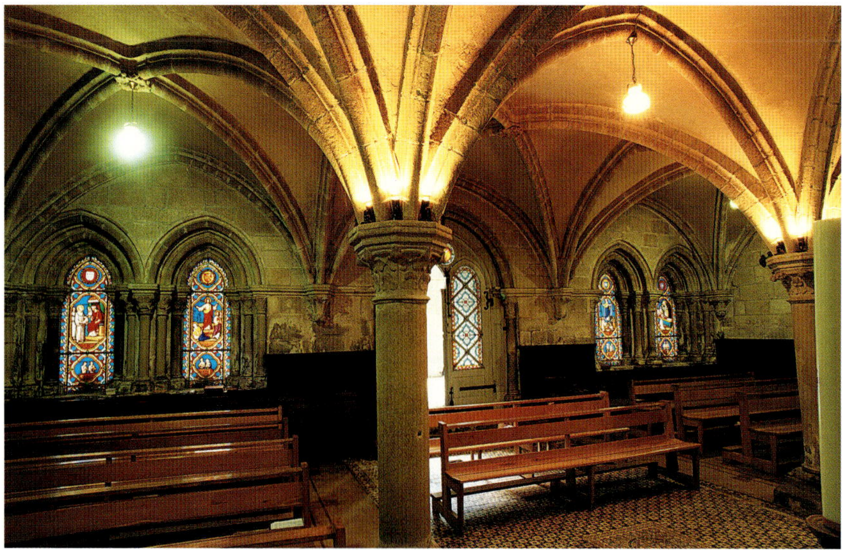
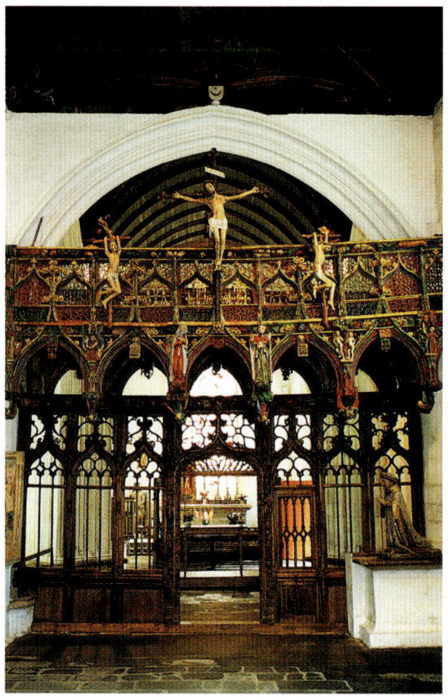
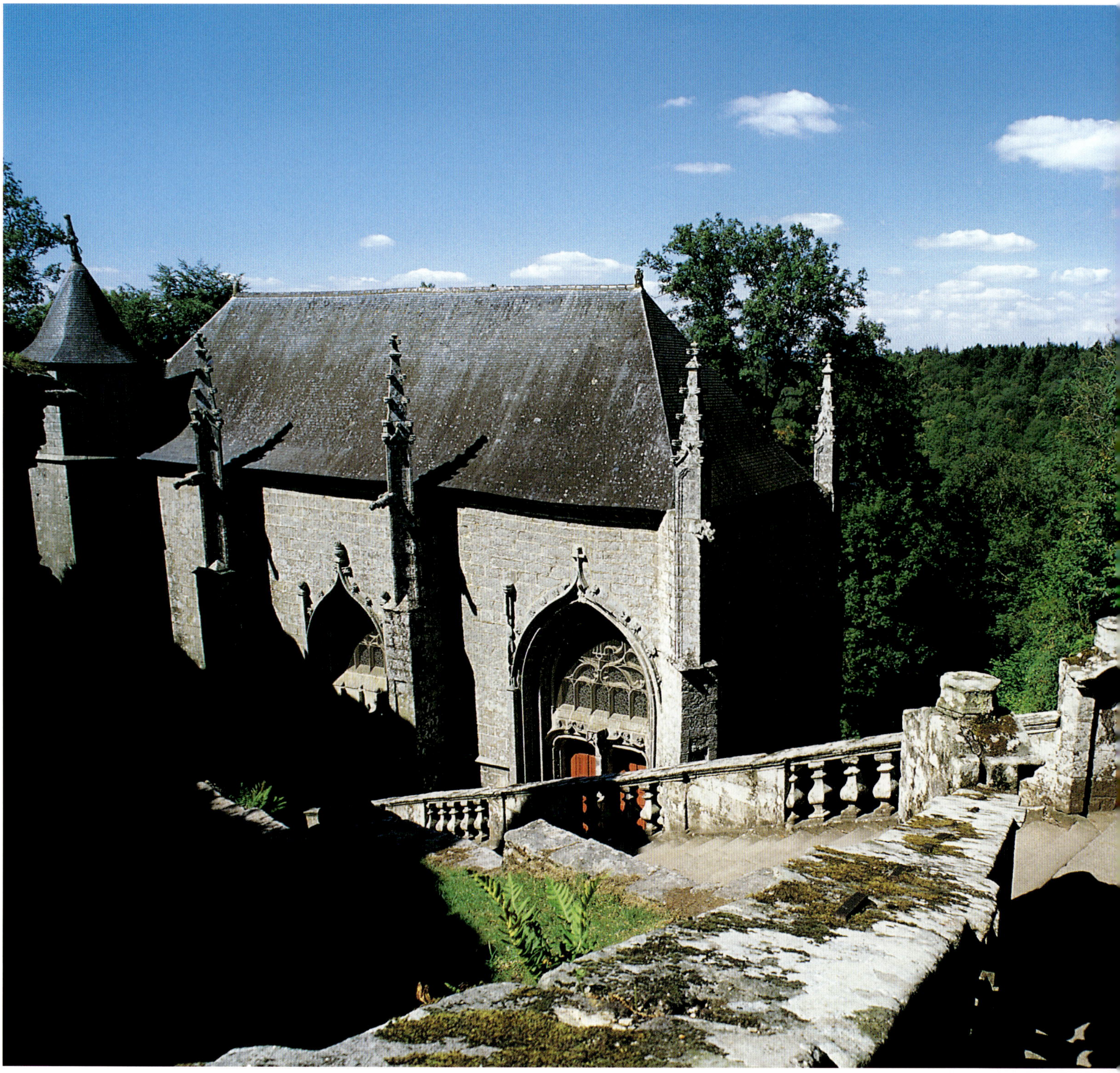

110 top left Although it belonged to the bishopric of Cornouaille, Langonnet, not far from the River Ellé, became part of Morbihan in the Revolution. The Cistercian abbey, founded in 1136 by Duke Conan III, includes the remains of a Roman nave and a 13th-century chapterhouse.

110 top right In Faouët, the polychrome wooden roodscreen in the chapel of Saint-Fiacre is a masterpiece in Gothic-flamboyant style, depicting animals, Biblical characters and scenes from everyday life. Next to the nave a series of statues portray scenes of the Temptation.

110-111 The chapel of Sainte-Barbe, in Le Faouët, built in 1498 in Gothic-flamboyant style on the sheer rock overhanging the River Ellé, is a celebration of the union of stone and wood.

111 top A detail of the roodscreen of Saint-Fiacre illustrating its vivid polychromy and richness of detail.

111 bottom The chapel of Saint-Fiacre in Le Faouët boasts one of the finest examples of the fortified bell towers that appeared in Brittany in the late 15th century.

Moving southeast, past Guémené sur-Scorff and Lignol, where the brave young marquis of Pontcallek was arrested, we come to Le Faouët which, although situated in the present-day district of Morbihan, is still part of the historical diocese of Cornouaille.

This parish, as well as having a magnificent 16th-century covered market, boasts two of the most beautiful chapels of Argoat. The 15th-century Chapel of Saint-Fiacre has one of the finest fortified bell-towers in Brittany; its *jubé* is virtually an embroidery in wood depicting the human sins, of which lust is actually represented as a *biniaouer*!

The other chapel is that of Saint Barbe, also in Gothic-flamboyant style, built on a rocky spur overlooking the green valley of Ellé, a true feast for the eyes and the soul.

Along the D769 we come to Langonnet, where Alan Stivell lived for some years with his family before moving to the region of Rennes.

The parish is worth a visit, especially for its abbey, which was founded in 1136 by Duke Conan III. Of the splendid Cistercian complex remains the magnificent Romanesque central nave, whose mysterious decorations "seem to appear out of the darkness of time — masks with enormous eyes gazing on the Other World, monsters that dance in a battle of wild beauty." (Marc Déceneux, La Bretagne romane.)

113 top left Like the German Black Forest, the Black Mountains of Brittany take their name from the colour of the omnipresent shale, or perhaps from the dark silhouettes of the conifers.

113 top right During the cold Winter days, when the trees are shrouded in a thick cloak of frost, the Black Mountains seem not to live up to their name. The Argoat region is the part of Brittany that has the most continental climate, with much harsher winters than in the coastal areas.

112 In the rugged landscape of the Black Mountains, at the beginning of the 20th Century, the last of the Breton wolves were hunted down and killed by the merciless Countess Vefa de Saint Pierre.

112-113 The Black Mountains are a range of mountains eroded by time, whose peaks reach the height of just 300 metres. In this photograph, taken from the borough of Laz, the pointed stumps of the reier can be seen.

At a short distance northward, from the heights of Glomel that still reverberate with the lyric and epic verses of the local bard Glenmor, to Karreg an Tan, which dominates the town of Gouézec, the Black Mountains align their "peaks." It takes the imagination of the local people to define as mountains this series of *menezioù*, hills with long, rounded tops alternated with *reier*, peaks of hard, jagged shale. It is around here, in the area of Toullaëron, the "culminating point," that in the early 20th-century Countess Vefa de Saint Pierre, a kind of Celtic Amazon who lived in the manor of Manez Cam, killed the last of the Breton wolves. At Gourin visitors should not be surprised to find in the Place de la Victoire a copy (more modest in size) of the famous Statue of Liberty of the port of New York. The "capital of the Black Mountains," in fact, is also the capital of emigration to America, which began in 1881 when Nicolas le Grand, not the Tsar of all the Russias but a humble tailor of Roudouallec, decided to seek his fortune on the far shores of the ocean. Today kinships are well-established, and every family of the Mountain has its own "American uncle." The association Bretagne-Trans-América, expertly run by the energetic Cristiane Jamet and Daniel Le Goff, who is also the organizer of the championship of musician duos *(biniou-bombarde)* that is held in the first weekend of September, is constantly in operation to maintain relations between the 4700 inhabitants of Gourin and the 7000 or so members of the Brittany-New York diaspora, and the others living in other American states or in Québec! Today the Black Mountains no longer echo with the noise of iron bars in the slate quarries which, represented the pride and wealth of the region. While the Société d'Exploitation des Ardoisières de Maël-Carhaix, with some ten employees, is considered an industry, and in Motreff, Honoré Maurice, last of the "Mohicans of the blue" (slate), exhausts himself tearing layers of *mordorè* (purplish-brown) slate from the hillside, at the same time the region of Poher does not rest on its laurels. The county of Conomor the Damned, a Breton version of the Irish Conchobar, and of King Morvan, who stood up to the Franks of Louis the Pious, is determined to stem the population 'haemorrhage' that has slowly but relentlessly been draining the *Kreizh Breizh* (the center of Brittany). The borough of Spezet has for years hosted the *Gouel Broadel ar Brezhoneg*, the National Festival of the Breton language, and its the bilingual signs on all the public buildings are a clear defiance of destiny. Here Breizh Co-op, with a staff of around forty, is dedicated to creating, publishing and circulating the *ne plus ultra* of the Breton culture. Carhaix, the ancient Celtic and later Gallo-Roman settlement of Vorgion, who rebelled against the imposition of stamped paper and proclaimed a (sadly short-lived) local republic. It was here, in fact, that the first Lycee de l'Ecole Bretonne immersive Diwan was set up and that autonomist mayor Christian Troadec intends to create an entire 'technopolis' of Breton culture, of which the Espace Culturel Glenmor, opened in 2001 and hosting so far the *Gouel levrioùe Breizh* (the Brittany Book Festival), may be considered the first brick.

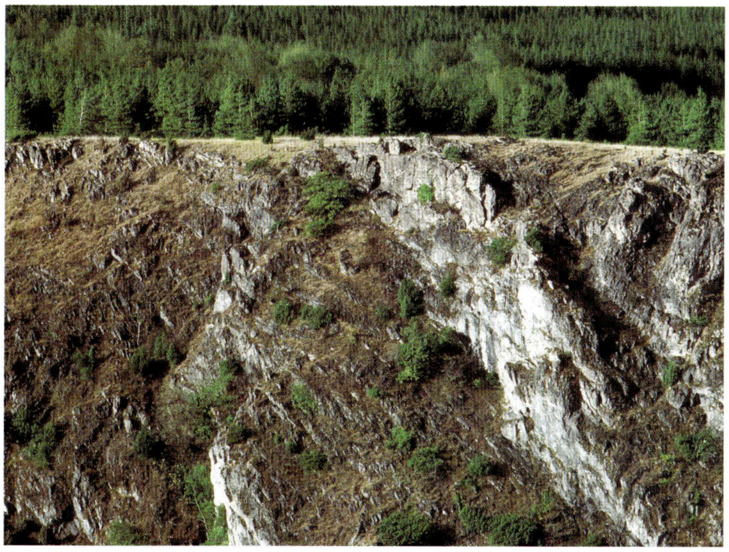

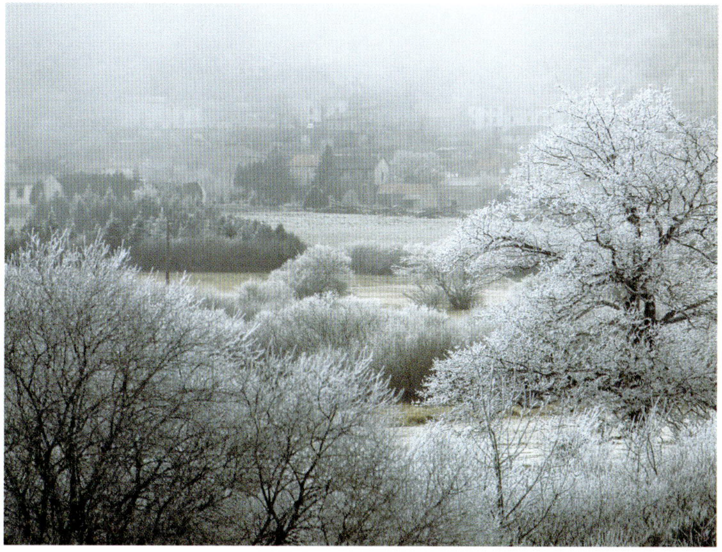

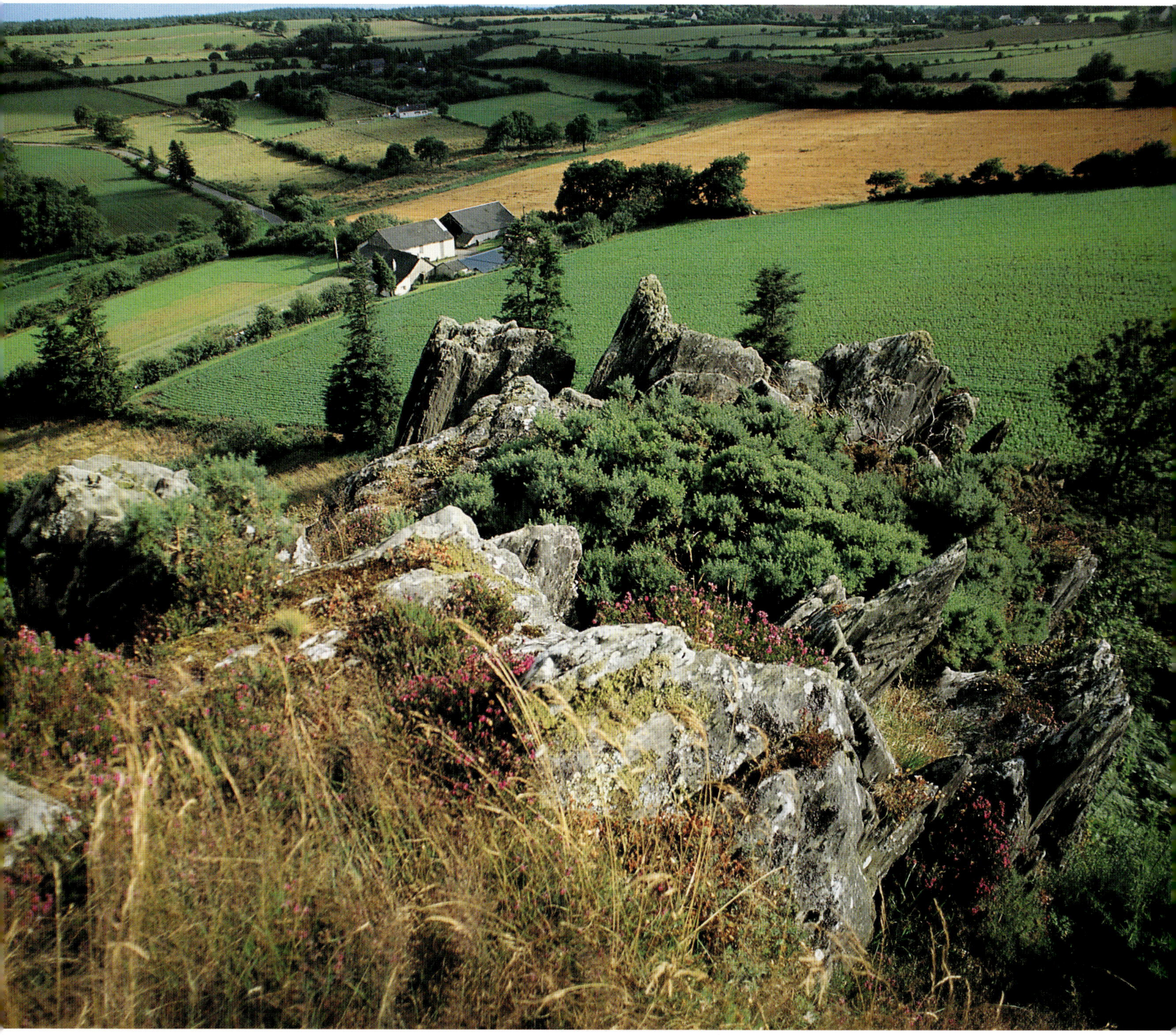

114 top On the peak of Menez Mikael, or Menez Kronan, as it was named in past ages after a Celtic god similar to Cromm Cruach, a bloodthirsy Irish deity, the chapel bearing the same name stands watch over the bleak range of the Monts d'Arrée and the 'infernal' marshland of Yeun-Ellez.

114 bottom The marshland of Yeun Ellez, the surface of which can be seen at the bottom of the picture, was where the ancient Bretons claimed the entrance to Hell lay. Here, in fact, the souls of traitors were hurled, personified by terrible black dogs in the bottomless pit.

114-115 Created in 1969, the Parc d'Armorique is one of the oldest regional parks in France. Stretching out from Ouessant and the archipelago of Molène on the west side as far as the borough of Guerlesquin, the park's 112,000 hectares of land and 60,000 hectares of sea include 39 boroughs.

To the northwest is the *kein Breizh,* "the backbone of Brittany." The mountain range begins with Menez Hom, a mountain that was once sacred and later holy, at the foot of which, in 1913, a farmer discovered a charming mask of the Dêua Brigantia, patron of the arts and goddess of fertility. The range then continues with the shale peaks of the Arrée Mountains and ends in the east with the moorlands of Mené, whose name means precisely "mountain." The rugged Mountains of Arrée, the tallest peak of which measures just 1,320 feet (400 m), are truly unique — a world of rock, pounded in winter by the violent *gwalarn* and where in the early morning long scarves of mist curl around Roc'h Trévézel, Menez Mikaël or Tuchen Gador. The region, it is true, is steeped in the presence of the Other World. Around the Lake of Brennilis roams the *Ankou,* a strange creature draped in a black sheet and carrying a scythe with the handle back to front for more easily tearing the souls from the living. The Washerwomen of the Night, at a stone's-throw from the entrance to the icy Hell of the Celts, as in the story by Émile Souvestre, watch out for drunks who linger on the road to force them to wring out their own funeral shroud. All around this area are the mysterious ponds of Yeun-Ellez — a name that instils fear in even the most daring. It was rumored, in fact, that in these bottomless depths wandered lost souls, caught between heaven and earth, in an endless search for eternal rest, and tormenting the living in an attempt to find relief. Evidently, through living so long with these creatures, the living must have finally tamed the dead and established good relations, since, for the past few years, the region has begun to come back to life.

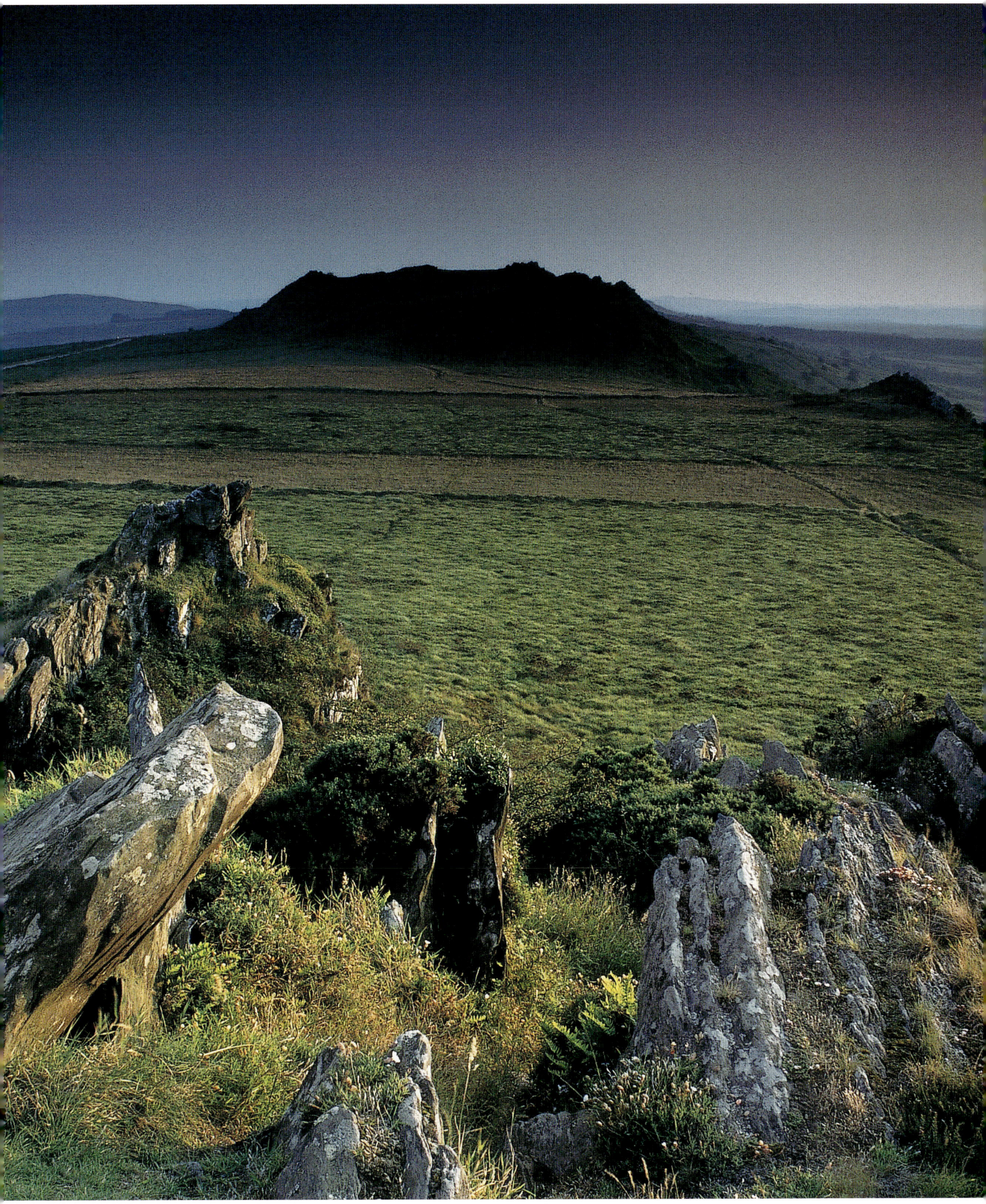

116 top The nurturing and protecting forest is the refuge of the deer, the totemic animal of the great Cernunos and the magician Merlin, as well as messenger from the Other World and the guide of souls.

116 bottom Wild boar, totemic animal of the Druids, are gradually coming back to inhabit the brushwood, thanks in part to the protection guaranteed by the institution of the founding Parc d'Armorique.

116-117 In Huelgoat, the 'tall wood', the Rivière d'Argent, whose waters have also returned after the closing down of the mines, surges around a turmoil of rocks. Here is where, according to legend, Ahès-Dahud had the lifeless bodies of her many lovers hurled.

Armorica Park, opened in July 1969, has its reception point in Menez Meur, with structures designed for the observation of wild animals — boars, wolves, deer, foxes, etc. — as well as domestic animals — Breton 'pie-noire' cows, Ouessant rams and the semi-wild horses of Brittany.

The Maison Cornec of Saint Rivoal, with its remarkable façade, known as "apothéis," houses an eco-museum dedicated to the history of rural architecture and farming implements.

In Commana, on the mountaintop, the covered passageway of Mougau (2000 B.C.) demonstrates that man has inhabited these mountains since remote times. This exceptionally well-preserved and impressive monument is made up of five slabs supported by 28 pillars. Inside several rock paintings are still visible, portraying spears, knives and three pairs of breasts of the Mother Goddess. The forest of Huelgoat, or "high forest," directly below the line of the mountaintop, lends an atmosphere of magic to the entire area. The magnificent Rivière d'Argent winds its way sensuously through a chaos of mossy rocks, in the shade of time-honored oaks and beeches still haunted by the presence of King Arthur. Certain ancient ruins in the area, claimed by local folk tradition to be an "encampment" of the providential king, are, in actual fact, the remains of an *oppidum*, a fortified site of the Osismes, dating back to the first century B.C., an age in which the populations of Armorica were at war with Caesar. According to legend (or, more simply, literature), moreover, here in this majestic forest was the abyss into which the damned soul of Ahés Dahud, the Queen of Ys, threw the lifeless bodies of her many lovers. On the northern slope of the Menez Arrée the charming ruins of the abbey of Relecq reflect in the waters of a shady lake. The church of the abbey, a 12th-century Romanesque building of typically Cistercian layout, was erected on the site of a monastery founded in the 6th century by Saint Tanguy and Saint Pol Aurélien.

117 top Argoat represents the holy alliance between ancient sacred buildings and the timeless woodlands, like the nemeton, *wood of the ancient Celts, where priests, poets and musicians gathered together to pay homage to the deities.*

119 top left In the complex of Lampaul-Guimiliau the two thieves writhe in agony alongside a completely serene Christ.

119 top right In spite of the 'nudity' of many statues in sacred art, we must remember that in the days of their splendor the images were 'dressed' in sparkling colors, like this group of sculptures inside the church of Lampaul-Guimiliau.

118 top The church of Saint Thégonnec houses a valuable Calvary and an ossuary, both of which date back to the 17th century. The church suffered severe damage in a fire in 1998, after which, fortunately, it was quickly restored.

118 bottom The parish church complex of Guimiliau contains what is perhaps the finest Calvary in Brittany. Created between 1581 and 1588, it portrays around two hundred characters, including the strange Katell Golet (Catherine the damned) with breasts swollen with desire and sin. In Brittany the complex is traditionally entered through the south porch, which can be seen in the picture.

118-119 The Calvary of Saint-Thégonnec, dating back to the early 17th century, is one of the most interesting in the famous circuit of parish church complexes. The group of sculptures portraying the "Abused Christ" has been created on the basis of a perfect symmetrical axis. The scene recalls the Breton Mysteries, representations of episodes in the life of Christ.

If there is an art in which the folk genius of Brittany — very often anonymous — has proved to excel, it is sacred art. This includes the parish church complexes, the dolmens, the menhirs and the lec'hioù, which represent the most ancient expressions of the intense spirituality of the Bretons. These complexes, which center around the parish churches, include the porch, where, until recently, the deceased of the clan were buried, the ossuary, situated on the west side facing the direction of the Celts' "Tir na n'Og," and a Calvary depicting scenes of the life of Christ.

Descending the slopes of the Mountains of Arrée, down on the plain of Léon is the triptych Guimiliau-Lampaul-Guimilau-Saint-Thégonnec, a truly marvelous work in granite, covered by a delicate embroidery of grey and golden lichens.

The Guimilau Calvary, constructed between 1580 and 1588, contains about 200 figures, including a serpent strangely resembling Morgana, the ancient goddess of the waters and Woman of the Afterlife, and a figure of the poor Katell Golet ("Catherine the Fallen"), an incarnation of lasciviousness condemned to suffer the torments of Hell.

The Calvary of Saint-Thégonnec, which dates back to 1610, depicts a particularly moving version of the humiliated Christ.

The most ancient complex is, however, that of Lampaul-Guimilau, which dates back to the early 16th century.

119

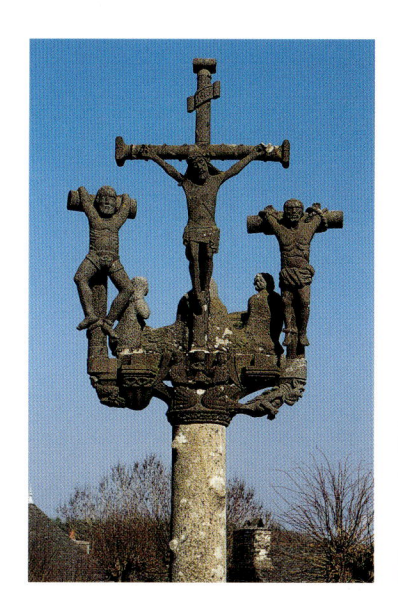

120

120 top left Built in a loop of the river Nançon, the castle of Fougères has witnessed some of the greatest events in the history of Brittany. Destroyed in 1166 by the English, it was rebuilt by the Bretons and subsequently occupied by the French in 1488. In 1793 it was the headquarters of the Chouan officers of Marquis de La Rouérie.

120 top right In Brittany there are over 900 saints, canonized more by public opinion than by the Vatican, which recognizes only one — Saint Yves.

120-121 Fougéres, situated on the borders of the region on an actual Breton "Maginot line," is a village of great interest. The fortress, with its thirteen towers, is one of the most impressive in Europe.

The picture shows the French-style gardens.

121 top Vitré, the city of historian Arthur Le Moyne de la Borderie, is part of a series of citadels on the border with Brittany's dangerous French neighbor. The castle, erected between 1380 and 1420, is a typical example of a fortress of the Hundred Years' War.

The eastern part of the region is a marchland, a borderland, which had to be constantly on the alert owing to the threat represented by its powerful neighbor. The area is characterized by the stone sentry posts that jealously guarded the borders of the dukedom, a place where proud-spirited men were always ready to take up arms and defend their hard-won rights.

In the town of Vitré narrow streets lined with 16th-century wattled buildings huddle sleepily around the citadel, which was erected between 1380 and 1420. Fougéres, on the road to Normandy, boasts an almost completely intact fortress which, in 1793, was the refuge of the Chouans of Marquis de la Rouérie.

The watchtowers of the castle of Combourg, purchased by a (priest) collector in 1793 at Saint Malo, still house the dreams — and fears — of François René de Châteaubriand, author of the *Mémoires d'outre tombe* and forefather of the great Romantic movement.

Of the fortified town of Saint Aubin du Cormier, once the scene of the fatal battle of 1488 and subsequently destroyed by the French in retaliation, there remains only a mass of ruins, evocatively reflected in the backwater.

121 center Behind the thick walls of the castle of Montmuran (12th-13th centuries) Bertrand du Guesclin, the famous constable of King Charles V, was knighted in 1354.

121 bottom The canal of Ille et Rance, which links the estuary of Vilaine on the Atlantic Ocean to that of Rance on the Channel, is part of a network of waterways extending for over 50 miles (800 km).

122

122 top left The little port of Dinan is an ideal place for relaxing, and from where visitors can take a boat ride down to Saint-Malo between the enchanting banks of the Rance.

122 top right The keep of Duchess Anne's castle in Dinan, dating back to the 14th century, has a series of remarkable trapdoors. The castle itself houses an interesting museum dedicated to the local handicrafts and the history of the city from its origins to modern times.

122-123 Built overlooking an inlet of the Rance, Dinan "like a swallow's nest" (Victor Hugo) is a true open-air museum with its numerous wattled buildings housing ancient workshops.

123 top The equestrian statue of Bertrand du Guesclin, in the square of the same name, demonstrates that to the inhabitants of Dinan King Charles V's constable was not a traitor in the pay of the King of France but rather a brave soldier who proved his worth in 1357 when the city, the English besieged.

123 bottom A close relative of the site known to archaeologists as the "Angevin porticoed dolmen," the site of Roche aux Fées in the borough of Essé, south-east of Rennes, is undoubtedly the finest of the Hexagon of France, with its blocks of red shale, the heaviest of which weighs a much as 50 tons.

At a distance of about 12 miles (20 km) to the west, overhanging the deep and winding River Rance (along which it is possible to take a boat ride as far as Saint Malo), lies Dinan, like "a swallow's nest," to use the words of Victor Hugo, one of the most beautiful and most complete of Brittany's fortified cities. It is worth dedicating at least a day to the town of Dinan, to admire the 13th-century ramparts, the evocative 14th-century castle, of which the tower of Coëtquen still stands, the impressive keep of Duchess Anne, the Basilica of Saint Saveur, erected in 1120 and the historical center, where there are ancient workshops with wooden beams and the characteristic benches outside. The best periods to visit the town are during the first fifteen days of July, when the prestigious Rencontres Internationales de la Harpe Celtique (International Celtic Harp Conventions) are held, or in September for the Medieval Festival.

At a short distance from the N137, which at the weekends brings the inhabitants of Rennes to the corsair city (today a seaside resort) of Saint-Malo, stands Bécherel, an ancient fortified town with characteristic granite buildings. For the past twenty years or so this town, like its Welsh cousin Hay-on-Wye, has been totally dedicated to the service of book-lovers and book-collectors, so much so as to earn the prestigious title of the first "book city" of the Hexagon (France).

Lastly, it would be quite inconsiderate towards the sharp-witted and hardworking inhabitants of the forests to leave Brittany and end this introductory journey without paying our respects to the most impressive, most prestigious and most enormous of the megalithic monuments of Argoat. The Roche aux Fées ("Fairies' Rock"), in the borough of Essé, is a magnificent dolmen which consists of a 63 feet (19 m) corridor made up of 42 rock masses covered with slabs, each weighing the modest total of 40 tons. This construction is so huge, in fact, that folk tradition attributes it to the fairies which, before they were driven out by "modern" civilization, inhabited in great numbers the forests of the region.

124 top left The Grand Théâtre, in the town hall square of Rennes, was built in 1836 in a Neo-classical style from the plans of architect Millardet.

124 bottom left The little square of Saint-Michel, with its coffee bars, restaurants and crêperie, is one of the liveliest places of Rennes.

124 top right As many as 900 wattled buildings were destroyed in the fire that caused extensive damage in Rennes in December of 1720.

124 center right Built between 1734 and 1742 by Jacques Gabrie, the Town Hall of Rennes is made up of two wings surmounted by a quaint 'clock tower'. In the center of the façade is a niche that until 1932 housed the "Statue of Shame."

124 bottom right The Parliament building, built between 1613 and 1655, the work of Parisian architect Salomon de la Brosse, was the first stone building in a city that until this time had been entirely in wood.

125 The 17th-century Benedictine convent of Saint-Georges is a clear indication of how the female religious orders prospered under the Ancien Régime.

Rennes, with the same importance for Argoat as Nantes has for Armor, is a city that is rich in history while at the same time keeping its sights firmly set on the future. With 212,000 inhabitants (375,000 the entire metropolitan area), the ancient Gallic and later Gallo-Roman settlement of Condate, city of the Redones, as well as the site of the last album of Asterix, Rennes is the smallest French city to have its own subway system. However, it became the seat of the regional government of Brittany only in 1554 with the setting up, after the annexation, of the Parliament of Brittany, the most important institution of the country, which defended the rights of the 'province' until it was abolished by the Revolution. Louis XIV, in order to punish the zealous jurists suspected of having stirred up, or at least encouraged, the insurrection of 1675 (known as the 'Stamped Paper Revolt') which began in Rennes and spread throughout Brittany, decided to 'exile' them to Vannes. It appears, however, that this institution retained its spirit of rebellion until at least the following century; the general proxy La Chalotais, in fact, was himself imprisoned by order of Louis XV. The parliament building, the work of Salomon de la Brosse, which became the seat of the Court of Appeal, disappeared very conveniently in flames in February 1994, during the violent clashes between fishermen and the police, and with it all the implicating documents about the AIDS-tainted blood scandal, along with the Gobelin tapestries portraying glorious scenes from the history of Brittany. Thanks in part to generous donations from Bretons themselves the building was restored to its original appearance, except for the structure; in addition, as one of the many examples of history turning a blind eye, the square of the "Hall" (of Justice) has taken back its old name — Place du Parlement (Parliament Square). Not far from this impressive building stands the Neo-Classic theatre where, in July 2001, composer Pierick Houdy made his debut with the magnificent opera *Anne de Bretagne*. The theater building looks as if it were endeavouring to become part of the façade of the Hôtel de Ville, in the center of which a mass of plants try desperately to disguise a surrealistic emptiness. In this niche, in fact, once stood the so-called "Statue of shame" portraying Brittany kneeling at the feet of the King of France, which was blown up in August 1932 by the underground national independence movement Gwenn ha Du, in occasion of the 400th anniversary of the annexation. Just outside the classical center, in the "medieval" districts of the city around place Sainte Anne and place des Lices, where tournaments were once held, are the finest examples of wattled houses in the whole of Brittany. Those, that is, that survived the terrible fire of 1720, in which more than one hundred people lost their lives and 8000 were left homeless.

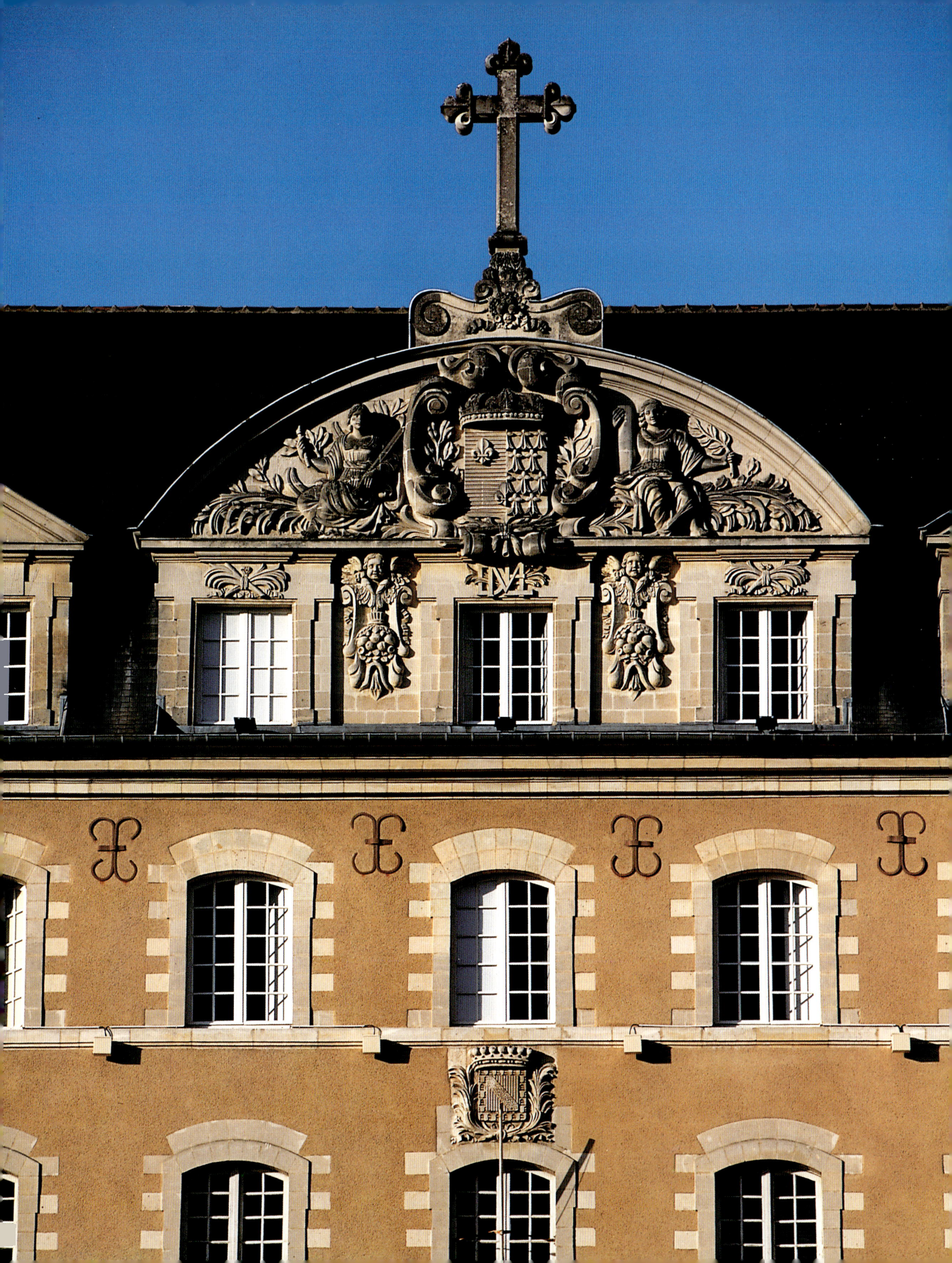

THE AWAKENING OF IDENTITY

126 In Brittany the traditional costume is undoubtedly considered a strong identifying element. To wear the time-honored headgear or waistcoat during important traditional events is an expression of the pride shared by a population that continues to refuse collective amnesia.

127 With the natural elegance of youth these young girls of the Fouesnant region show off a costume that enhances their gracefulness. The combination of the giz-Fouën bonnet and the collar make this costume of the Rias region one of the most attractive in Brittany.

Thanks to the laboriousness with which the Bretons, albeit peacefully, left their mark throughout Europe, roamed the seas, settled in the cities of the world and hung around ports across the globe (in a diaspora which, although smaller in numbers than those of the Irish or Scots, was nevertheless considerable) they quickly became distinguished as a population, and known as a people whose identity was bound inseparably to its soul. The identity of the Bretons was obviously related to their language, the last Celtic language of the continent which, although it is still spoken today by around 300,000 people, risks dying out before the next century if the French government fails to ratify and apply as soon as possible the European Map of Regional Languages and Language Minorities.

Naturally, the rich and multiform identity of the Bretons is expressed also in their traditional costumes, the extraordinary variety of which dates back to the 18th century, although their heyday was in the mid-19th century, when they were immortalised in the paintings of Perrin, Grignel and Lalaisse. Each individual community was distinguished by the women's hairstyles, the height of the men's hats, the size of the belt buckles and the width of the *bragoù-braz*, the strange, baggy trousers that were worn with leggings. The extravagance of these costumes was matched only by the veritable orgy of colours in which they appeared — the violent reds and deep mauves of Plougastel's costumes contrasting with the stunning burnt gold of those of Bigouden. A race of lords, we might be tempted to remark while viewing the impressive showcases at the Musée Départemental Breton of Quimper, if we did not know that those magnificent "costumes" were in actual fact worn for the festivities of the rural aristocracy while, in the same period, the farm laborers went about in rags. Today, the traditional costumes are worn only by the eldest women and only in certain places, such as the peninsula of Plougastel or Bigouden, or for events that are now defined as "folklore festivals."

However, thanks to certain idealistic and generous individuals, such as R.Y. Creston, a distinguished member of the *Seiz Breur* art school, several of these garments have been immortalized as symbols. The famous *kabig*, for example, before being appropriated by the students, was actually the working attire of the fishermen of Lyons. Over the past decade a number of young and talented fashion designers (such as Val Piriou of Quimper or Christian Le Drezen of Bigouden, who prematurely passed over to the Paradise of the Celts after promising international debuts), have adopted the traditional Breton motifs and models and adapted them to the brilliant imagery of high fashion. Besides its language and its costumes, however, Brittany is also famous for its dances, which today are enjoying a popularity that is perhaps even greater than ever before. Immediately after the war, when all Breton political activities were strictly forbidden, the energy of the young people found expression in cultural pursuits. The Celtic clubs (the first of which was created in Paris in 1911) underwent a true explosion. On his part, Loeiz Roparz, a young teacher in the "mountain" area of Pollaouenn, had the idea of "modernizing" the old, rural

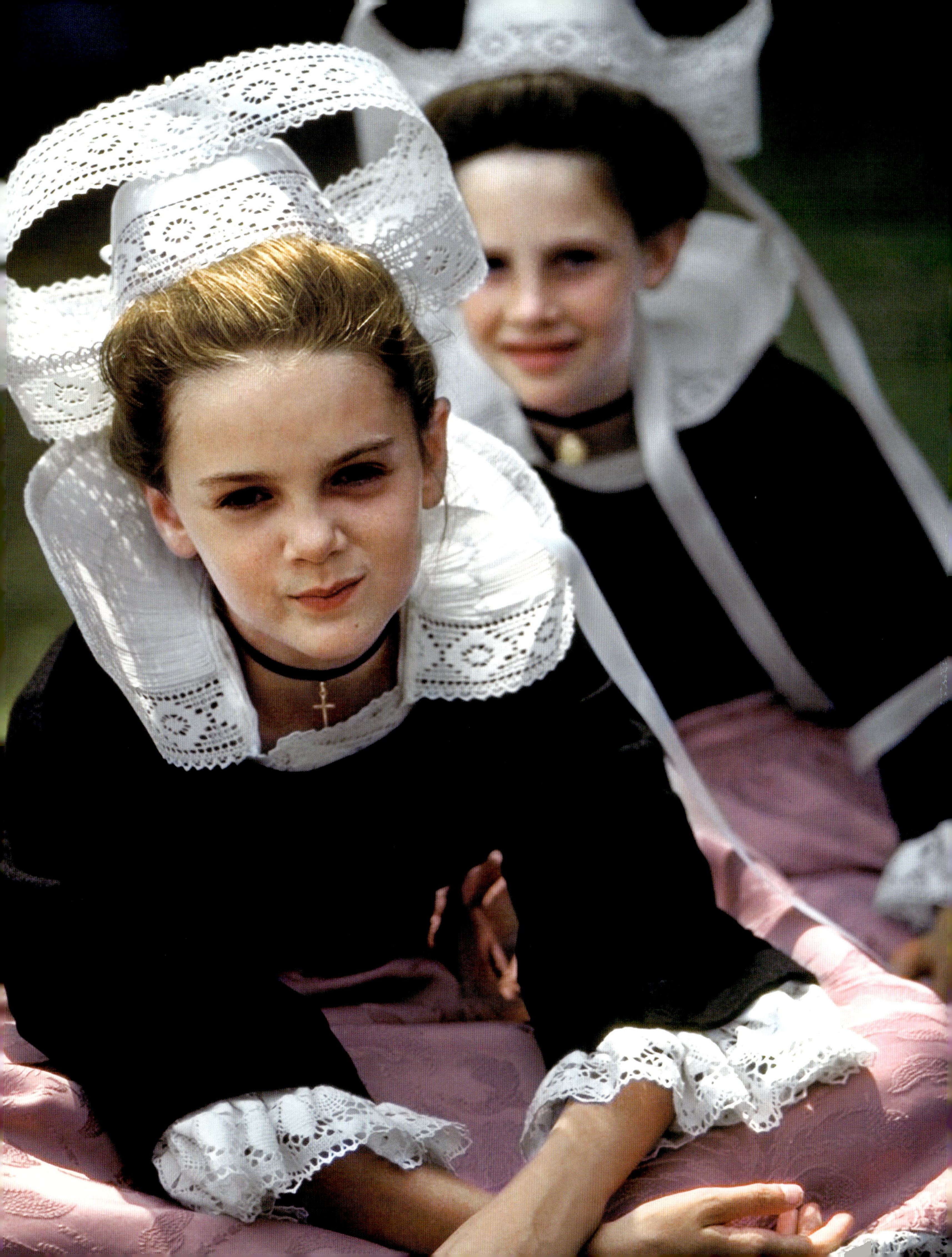

128 top left A local girl from Pont-l'Abbé wears with pride her typical pays bigouden (Brittany) bonnet; this headgear is such an emblematic element that it has become the symbol of the extraordinary variety of Breton traditional dress.

night-time festivals known as *fest-noz*. He was the first to organize evening dances in halls, with the dancers separated from the singers, who were set on a makeshift stage and eventually even equipped with microphones. Since then, the "Breton dances," as they came to be called, have enjoyed overwhelming success, kindling an enthusiasm that affected city and country folk alike and producing true "stars" such as the Goadec sisters or the Morvan brothers.

Today, these "night-time parties" attract every Saturday a public composed of all age groups and all social categories, who dance together the *gavotte* or form Circassian circles to the sound of the *kann ha diskann* — the famous *tuilé* singing of the *Kreizh Breiz* — accompanied by the inseparable bombarde-bagpipe duo. Besides the traditional *festoù-noz* there are many other occasions for dancing, including innumerable festivals, in which the Celtic clubs show off their skill and initiate tourists into such traditional dances as the *kost-ar-c'hoat* or the *an-dro*. While the Cornouaille Festival at Quimper is without doubt (as its president Jean-Michel Le Viol claims) the "flagship of the Breton culture," in summer months there are an astounding number of events throughout Brittany, each with its own particular identity: Hortensias in Perros-Guirec, Saint-Loup de Guingamp, dedicated to folk dances, Fleurs d'Ajonc at Pont-Aven, in the region of Gauguin and at Concarneau, Les Filets Bleus, a great folk event that began in the early 20th century as a way to help the fishermen who had been impoverished by the disappearance of the sardine shoals. Of all these, however, it is the Festival Interceltique of Lorient, which has managed to avoid the double trap of folklore and closing-down, that best represents the Breton culture today.

If the folk dances of Brittany can be said to be one of its finest expressions, this is even truer of its music and songs. The Bretons have been singing, in fact, ever since the traditional motives, recited by the bards to the sound of the *telenn* (Celtic harps) or the *crwth*, enchanted courts throughout Europe with the story of the unhappy love between Tristan and Isenlt or the adventures of the valiant knights of the Round Table. The Breton harp actually disappeared from the continent in around the 14th century and was replaced by a coarser, less refined copy, which went on to incarnate the seductive power of the music of Brittany. Right from the 18th century the combination of the *biniou*, small bagpipes with a high tessitura and very short pipes, and the bom-

128 top right For the Filets Bleus festival of Concarneau this girl is wearing the costume of the "salters" of the Guérande region, which owes its prosperity precisely to the salt trade.

128-129 Elegant collars resembling gulls' wings, bonnets of white lace on sky-blue satin coëff-blew, *bodices finely embroidered in iridescent colours — these are the "broom flowers" of Pont-Aven that were so admired by Paul Gaugin and his "nabis" friends.*

129 top A woman wearing the traditional dress of Bannaleg. The bodice is plain black and the collar is much more modest than that of the costume of nearby Pont-Aven.

129 bottom At the embroiderers' festival in Pont-l'Abbé, these young men pose in their Quimper costumes. The men's baggy, puffed trousers, known as bragoù-braz, *date back to the 19th Century and were worn in Cornouaille and the region of Vannes until 1900.*

130 left At Brec'h, in Bro Gwened (region of Vannes), "pardonneurs" abandon themselves to the sound of the bombarde-biniou (Breton bagpipes) duo, an essential element of all folk celebrations since the 18th century.

130 top right The boest an diaoul, or "devil's box" made its appearance in Brittany at the end of the 19th century. After being overshadowed, in postwar years, by the revival of the bombarde-biniou duo and the great comeback of the Highland bagpipes, the diatonic accordion once again became popular, especially with the younger generations.

130 bottom right This musician in Quimper dress, with his biniou-vraz, or "large Scottish bagpipes," is an illustration of the Bretons' infatuation for the "windbag" of their Gaelic cousins, which became popular in Brittany after Polig Monjarret, Dorig Le Voyer and Robert Marie brought the Bogadeg ar Sonerien *(Players' Assembly) to the baptismal font in 1943.*

131 The Festival of Cornouaille, initiated in 1923, is defined by its president, Jean-Michel Le Viol, as "the flagship of Breton culture." The event is an excellent opportunity for showing off the various costumes of the land of King Gradlon, some of which are the most striking of all Brittany.

barde, a medieval oboe usually made from box-wood, has been synonymous with Breton folk music. After a considerable decline just before the war, this music, which was mainly an expression of the farming culture, later underwent an extraordinary revival, gaining popularity from city to city thanks to the *Bogadeg ar Sonerien* (Assembly of Pipers). The stroke of genius of these musicians was to create, on the Scottish model, a Breton pipe band, which was initially called a *clique* (gang, band), then later band, followed by *bagad-sonerion*, until in 1950 it became simply *bagad*. The music of Brittany would not have such a widespread popularity today if it had not been for the efforts and perseverance of Jord Cochevelou, a native of Gourin, who, in his Paris exile, decided to bring back to life the ancient *telenn*, the harp of the Celts. His son Alan, who was later to become famous with the surname of Stivell (the "spouting spring"), played this harp for the first time at the Maison de la Bretagne in Paris, in November of 1953, winning overnight success. However, the turning point in Alan's career was the concert at the Olympia in January 1972. This marked the beginning of a revolution, manifest by the elated Breton youth of the capital, who went around singing at the top of their voices old battle songs like *An Alarc'h* and the famous *Suite Sud Armoricaine*. The way was paved for the rebirth of Brittany and the rediscovery of its identity. Following in the footsteps of Stivell came those whom Xavier Grall, from his refuge of Bossulan, affectionately defined as "the enlightened" — the guardians and the seers, those who imagine a future that meets the needs of the country: Dan ar Braz, who brought together the Celtic heritage, Myrdhin, Kristenn Nogués, Triskell, Tri Yann, Gweltaz ar Fur, Kirjuhel, Kerguiduff and Servat, whose "Blanche hermine" was to become a second national anthem. It is impossible to give a faithful description of the Breton people without including their feeling for the sacred, the ardent and all-consuming spirituality that throughout the ages has remained the most characteristic feature of the Celts.

Theirs is a spirituality that, since time immemorial, has always found its best expression through the popular, clan-oriented veneration of a myriad of saints (nine hundred, according to Gwenc'hlan le Scouézec), of which only one, the national saint Saint-Yves, is recognized and listed among those of the Catholic Church.

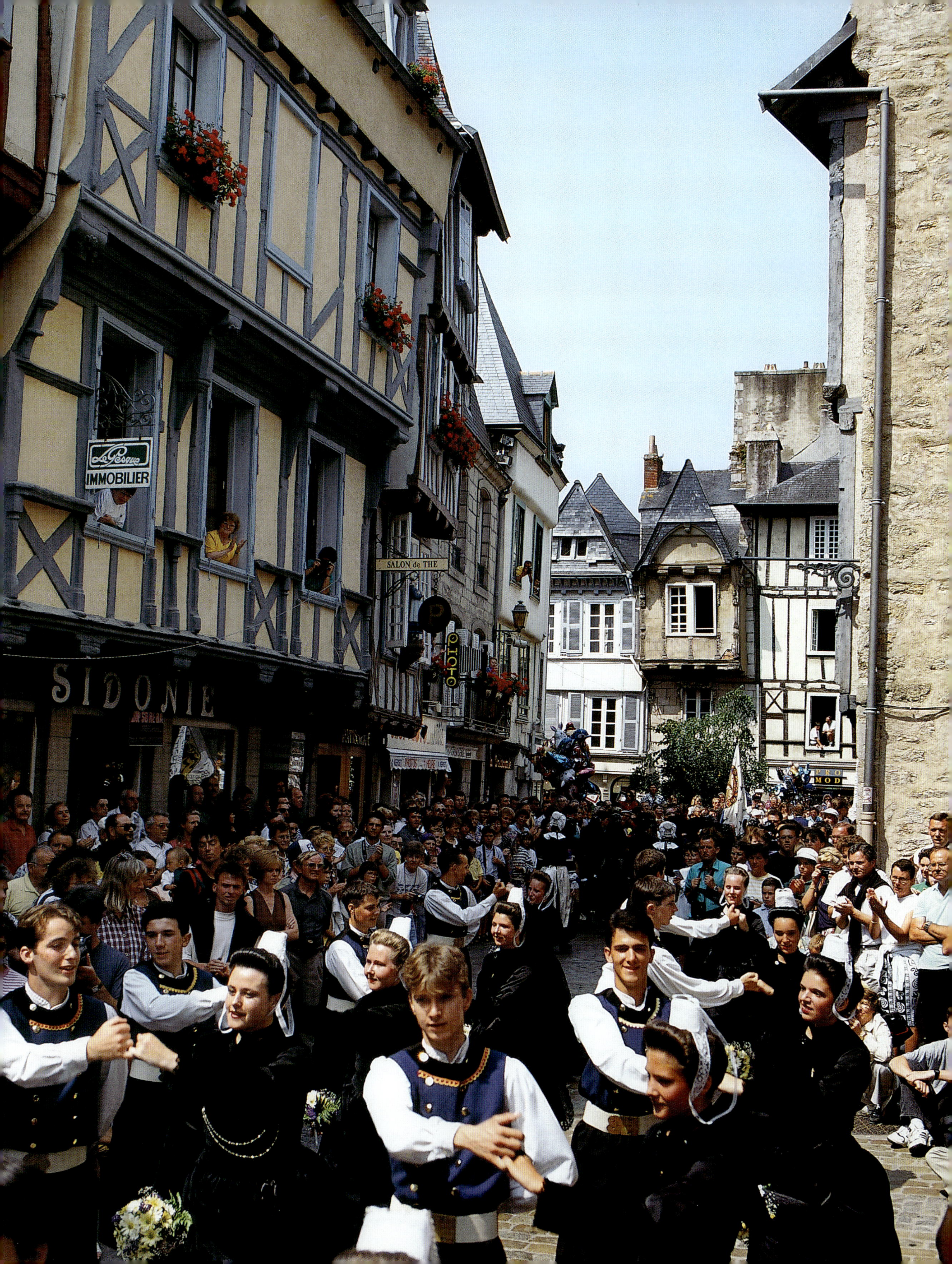
IMMOBILIER
SALON de THE
SIDONIE

132 top The Troménie is actually the revival of a procession dating back to the days of the Druids (or perhaps even earlier) and corresponding to a precise solar calendar. All along the sacred route small "altars" are placed, decorated with flowers and vegetables, in honour of saints who are totally unknown to the Catholic Church.

132 bottom Standards are a glorious and essential part of the pardons. Mainly written in the language of Brittany, they represent a sign of prosperity and a symbol of identity.

133 Saint-Ronan, along the Troménie route on the sacred mountain, where in August the ancient Celtic celebrations of Lugnasad-Lugunassatis are held. Descending along the path lined with ferns and broom, the women and girls seeking to have children sit on the gazez vean, *the ancient fertility stone.*

The others, such as Arzhel, Miliau, Mélar, Nona, Gireg, Maodez, Efflam, Enora and Tudwal, are today basically unknown, their origins lost in the collective memory and the dawn of time.

It is not difficult, however, to discern behind the mask of Santez Anna, Patron Saint of the Bretons, the smile of Deva Anna, the Great Mother of the Celts and the gods, just as the great Cernunos can be seen in the polychrome paintings depicting old Cornely, the horned protector of animals venerated in Carnac.

To cater to all these "idols" of this little world of stone and wood there had to be festivals, ceremonial worship, tribal adoration. Thus the processions known as *"pardons"* were created, which, after being abolished during the "enlightenment" of the French Revolution, became extremely popular again in the 19th century with the Romantic movement, the rehabilitation of the supernatural and the triumphant mania for the Celtic culture. Extremely picturesque, these processions represented a veritable celebration of the mystic and many of them, such as the famous *troménie* of Locronan, reintroduced ancient sacred Celtic and solar routes.

After the *Tan Tad* (the Purifying Fire), also of ancestral heritage, and the great procession, the "pardon" gave way to the profane festival. Anatole Le Braz describes the "pardon" of Sainte Anne La Palud as follows: "A kind of nomadic city took shape before our eyes. As in the days when the herding populations migrated, as far as the eye could see there were tents of all colors and all shapes, clustered in groups and rippling in the wind, resembling a Barbarian camp or, better still, the breaking of the waves on the sea."

After the religious ceremonies there are banquets, Breton wrestling, and dances accompanied by the music of *biniou* and *talabard* players, who blow so hard on their instruments as to burst their cheeks. From a sacred celebration the "pardon" is capable of transforming into a Dionysian orgy, or a great hullaballo.

These parish, diocesan or national rallies are, naturally, also occasions for dressing up and showing off the most colorful costumes. In around the mid-19th century Emile Souvestre gave the following commentary: "(it) gathered an immense crowd together in Lannion. All the parishes of the Côtes-du-Nord had sent their representatives. There were the roses of Trégor, whose slender hats recalled the shape of the American piraguas; the hot-blooded maidens of Lamballe with imploring eyes and inviting lips, with their flowing, black locks that fell from their Italian bonnets; there were the girls of Lannion, who blossomed beneath the locks of hairstyles resembling the wings of a moth.

Following these were the men of Menez Bré, with their garments of white cloth, their long hair and enormous fire-hardened clogs."

After a short period of estrangement these events, so deeply-rooted in folk tradition, are once more gaining popularity with the reassertion of the Breton culture, as it rediscovers its original vocation and the almost pagan identity of which the renowned philosopher Ernest Renan was so fond.

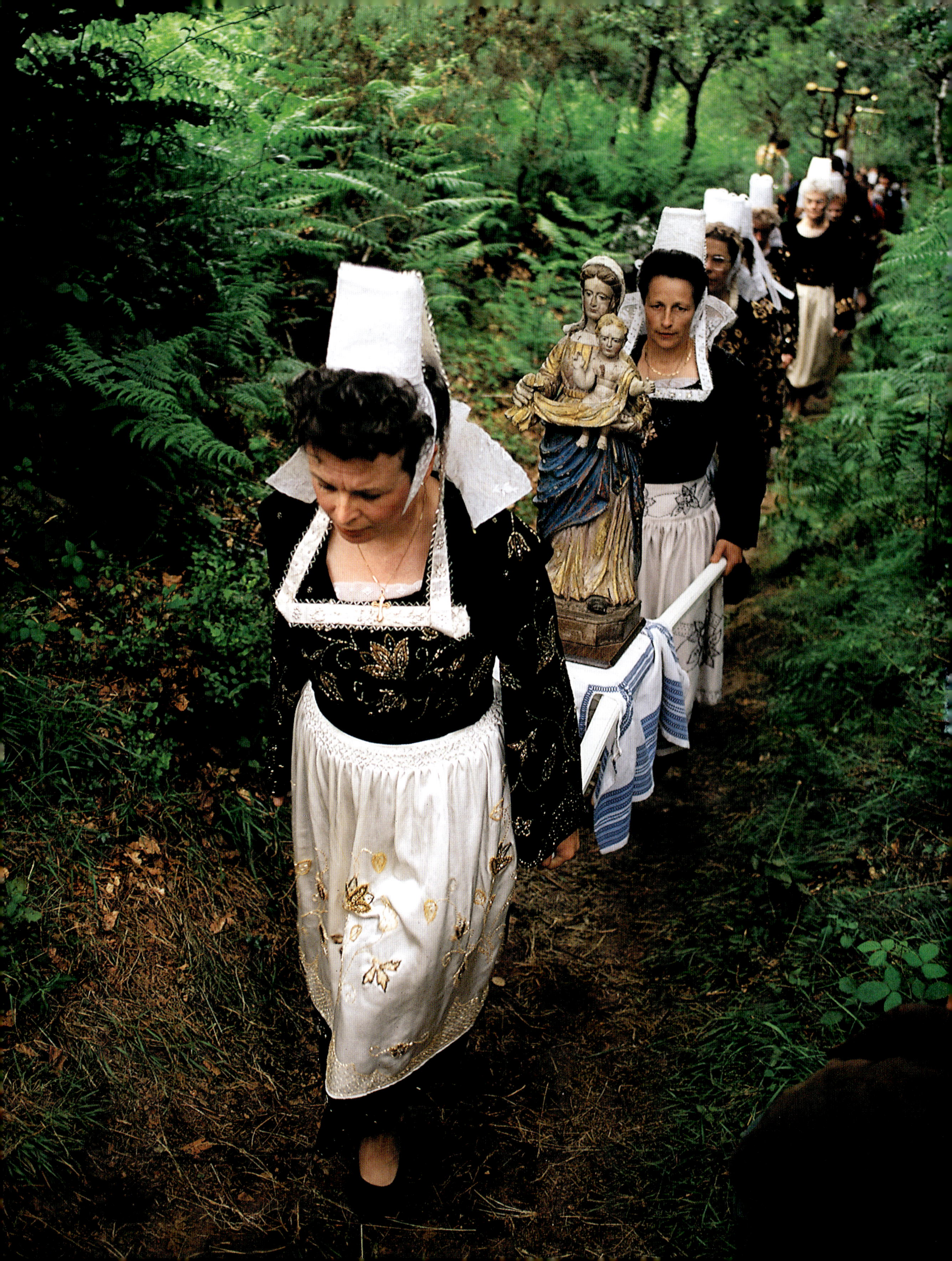

INDEX

c = *caption*

A
Abbé Poisson, 23
Ahès Dehud, 8, 40, 78, 78c 116 116
Ambrosius Aurelianus, 26
Ana, goddess, 18
Angles, the, 25, 25c
Anglo-Saxons, the, 28c
Angouleme, Francis of, 31
Anjou, 28
Anne of Brittany, 30, 31c, 95, 109
Antille, 40
Arcouest, 62
Argoat, 11, 64c, 99, 102, 111, 112, 112c, 117c, 123, 124
Armor, 11, 58c, 64c, 99, 102, 106, 124
Armorica, 8, 11, 20c, 21, 21c, 25, 25, 25c, 26, 28, 40, 93, 114c, 116, 116c
Armoricans, 22c, 23, 25
Arrée Mountains, the, 12, 114, 114c, 118
Arthur, 25, 37, 40, 69, 99c, 116
Arvernia, 23
Arzhel, 132
Asterix, 124
Atlantic Ocean, 12, 42, 46, 60, 121c
Audierne, bay of, 9c
Aulne, 12
Auray, 28c
Ausone, 52c
Ausonio, 23
Aval, 69
Avalon, 18, 40
Avangour, 30
Aven, 12, 82
Avranchin, 28

B
Bains sur Oust, 26
Ballon, 26
Ban de Bénoic, 101c
Bannaleg, 129c
Bannockburn, 26
Barnenez, 18, 73, 73c
Bassan, 70, 70c
Batz, island of, 12, 75, 75c
Batz-sur-Mer, 93, 93c
Baud, 105
Beauport, abbey of, 60, 60c
Bécherel, 123
Becker, Roland, 102
Bélénos, divinity, 105
Belle-Île, 12, 46c, 82, 82c, 86c
Bernard, Emile, 82, 97c
Berthou, Yves, 35
Betton, 9c
Bidard de la Noé, M., 35
Bieuzy, 106
Bigouden, 126
Bilfot, 60c
Binic, 42, 58, 58c
Birlmot, 62c
Black Mountains, the, 12, 84c, 112, 112c
Blain, castle of, 93c
Blanqui, 73
Blavet, 12, 105, 105c, 106
Bon-Repos, abbey of, 106
Bordeaux, 23, 40
Bossulan, 130
Botrel, Théodore, 60
Bourraeu, Maison du, 9c
Brandan, 40
Brec'h, 130c
Bréhat, island of, 12, 60c, 62, 62c, 75c
Bréhec, 60, 60c
Breizh, 18
Brennilis, lake, 114
Brest, 12, 37c, 40c, 44, 44c, 46, 62c, 75c
Bretons, 8, 11, 32c, 33c, 36, 40, 41c, 42, 42c, 46c, 53c, 114c, 118c, 121c, 126, 132
Brigneau, 82
Brignogan, 12, 75
Brioc, 25
Britons, 25, 25c, 26
Bro Gwened, 106, 130c
Bro Waroc, 26, 91c
Broca, Philippe de, 56
Brocéliande, forest of, 8, 99, 99c, 100, 100c, 102c
Brosse, Salomon de la, 124, 124c
Brouscon, Guillaume, 40
Bruce, Robert, 26
Brutus, Caius Junius, 22c, 23, 88
Bu, chateau du, 102
Buguélès, 66

C
Cadoual, George, 32, 35, 41c
Caledonia, 75c
Calloc'h, Yann-Ber, 86, 86c
Camaret, 46c
Camors, 105
Cancale, 13, 46, 51c
Cap du Raz, 12, 78, 78c
Cap Fréhel, 13, 56
Capetingi, 32
Carantec, 12, 73
Carhaix, 23, 37c, 112
Charles of Luxembourg, 30
Charles the Bald, 26, 27c
Charles V, 28, 30, 121c, 123c
Charles VIII, 30, 31c, 95, 105, 105c
Carnac, 12, 18, 88, 88c, 132
Cartier, Jacques, 8c, 40, 41c, 53
Cassiterides, isles of, 23
Castennec, 105
Cellamare, 32
Celti, 18, 53c, 88c, 99c, 114, 117c, 118, 130
Cenomans, the, 21c
Cernunos, divinity, 18, 88c, 100c, 114c
Champs-Elysées, 35c
Chardronnet, 28
Charles de Blois, 28c
Chateaubriand, François René de, 53, 53c, 121
Chateaubriant, 13
Chouans, 33c, 41c
Claudia, daughter of Anne of Brittany 30
Clisson, Olivier de, 109c
Clodoveo, 26c
Cocheveleu, Jord, 130
Coet-Bihan, 105
Coetquen, 123
Colombe, Michel, 95
Combourg, 53c, 121
Commana, 116
Comper, castle, 100, 100c
Comper, lake, 101c
Conan III, 111, 111c
Concarneau, 12, 37c, 82, 82c, 129, 129c
Conchobar, 112
Conguel, 18c
Conlie, 35c
Conomor, 112
Conquet, 40
Corbière, Tristan, 35, 73c, 75, 75c
Corelleau, Nicole, 82
Coriosoliti, 21
Cork, 75c
Cornely, 132
Cornovaglia, 12, 26, 35, 44c, 82, 82c, 84c, 88c, 99c, 111, 111c, 129, 129c, 130c
Costaérès, 66
Cotentin, 28
Cornes d'Armor, 12
Cote d'Emeraude, 56c
Cottereau, Jean, 99
Couesnon, 28
Creac'h, 11c, 77, 77c
Creston, R. Y., 126
Cromm Cruach, 114c
Crozon, 40c, 46c

D
D'Argentré, Bertrand, 26
D'Avaugour, Alain, 60c
Dahouet, 58, 58c
Dan ar Braz, 130
Daol, 77
Daoulas, Logonna, 44
De Clisson, Olivier, 93c
De Foix, Marguerite, 95
De Grève, Lieue, 66
De Keratry, Emile, 35
De Kermatin, Yves Helori, 69c
De la Fontenelle, Guy Eder, 99
De la Tour, Georges, 97c
De l'Estourbeillon, Régis, 35c, 36
Déceneux, Marc, 111
Delacroix, Eugène, 97c
Denez, Goulven, 78
Deva Ana, *see also* Ana, 46c
Dibenn, 73, 73c
Dinan, 13, 53c, 123, 123c
Dinard, 13, 28, 56
Dixmude, 37c
Doelan, 82
Dol, 28
Domnonée, 26
Douarnenez, 12, 40c, 42, 42c, 46, 78, 78c, 82
Douarnenez, bay of, 25
Dougall, 70
Doumergue, Gaston, 44c
Druids, 116c
Drummond Castle, 77
Du Four, Antoine, 31c
Du Guesclin, Bertrand, 121c, 123c
Dugay-Trouin, 40, 41c, 53

E
Efflam, 25, 69, 132
Ellé, 111, 111c
English Channel, the, 11c, 12, 25, 28, 46, 58c, 121c
Enora, 132
Erdre, 13
Erispoè, 28
Essé, 123, 123c
Estienne, Charles, 11

F
Faouet, 105c, 111, 111c
Faouet, Marion du, 99
Faroer, islands of, 77c
Phoenicians, the, 23
Fiandre, 40
Finistère, 12
Flaubert, Gustave, 58
Fleisher, Richard, 56, 56c
Fleuriot, Léon, 25c, 26
Fort-la-Latte, 56c
Fouéré, Yann, 36, 37
Fouesnant, 126c
Fougères, 13, 121, 121c
François II, 30, 31c, 93c, 95, 105c, 109
French, the, 28, 30, 40, 121, 121c
Franks, the, 25, 26, 27c, 112
France, 8, 12, 23, 28, 29c, 31c, 32, 36, 40, 42c, 53, 88, 91, 95, 95c, 109, 114c, 123, 123c
Frehel, lighthouse of, 56c
Fromveur, 77
Fundy, bay of, 46, 48c

G
Gabrie, Jacques, 124c
Gacilly, 102
Gauls, the, 21c, 23
Gaul, 23, 25c
Gambetta, Léon, 35
Garangeau, Simon, 56
Gauguin, Paul, 82, 129, 129c
Gautier, Alain, 40
Gavrinis, island of, 18c
Gicquel, Roger, 39c
Gireg, 132
Glénans, islands of, 82c
Glenmor, 82, 112
Glomel, 112
Glot, Claudine, 99
Goelo, 40, 60c
Gouézec, 112
Gourin, 12, 112, 130
Goursez, 35

Gourvennec, Alexis, 55c
Gouyon-Matignon, 56, 56c
Gradlon, 8, 25, 78, 78c, 130c
Grall, Xavier, 53c, 82, 130
Grand Bé, 53, 53c
Granville, 13, 46
Grignel, 126
Groix, island of, 12, 25, 82, 82c, 86, 86c
Guéméné sur Scorff, 111
Guer, 102
Guérande, 93, 129c
Guerledan, lake of, 106, 106c
Guerlesquin, 114c
Guillemer, 58
Guilvinec, 12, 82, 82c
Guimilau, 118
Guingamp, 35, 62, 64c, 129
Guyonvarc'h, Christian, 99
Gwalarn, 114
Gweltaz ar Fur, 130
Gwenc'hlan le Scouezec, 11, 66, 105, 130
Gwenn ha Du, 124
Gwent, 23
Gwyned, 23

H
Hallstatt, culture of, 20c
Hasting, 69
Hay-on-Wye, 123
Henry VII, 105
Hervé, 66
Hervily, 33c
Highlands, 130c
Hirtius, 23
Houdy, Pierick, 124
Huelgoat, 12, 116
Hugo, Victor, 11, 123, 123c

I
Île aux Moines, 70
Île de Noirmoutier, 13
Île de Ouvessant, 11c, 12
Île de Seine, 12
Île Louet, 73, 73c
Îles de Glénan, 12
Ille et Rance, 121c
Ille et Vilaine, 9c
Indut, 25
Ingres, Auguste, 97c
Ireland, 18c, 28, 36, 37, 75c
Irish, the, 36, 37
Iroise, sea of, 40c, 46
Iroise, bridge of, 44c
Isolde, 129

J
Jacob, 36
Jaffrenou, Taldir, 35
Jamet, Cristiane, 112
Jean of Rohan, 109, 109c
Jean II of Rohan, 106c, 109
Jean III, 109
Jean IV, 28, 53, 69c, 93
Jean V, 28
Josselin, 13, 109, 109c
Julius Caesar, 22c, 23, 88, 116

K
Karreg an Tan, 112
Katell-Golet, 118, 118c
Kemper, 99
Keralio, manor of, 102c
Kerguiduff, 130
Kerity, 60c
Kerlescan, 88, 88c
Kermario, 88, 88c
Kerpont, 62c
Kersauzon, 40
Kirjuhel, 130
Konwoion, 103c
Korrigan, 60c
Kreizh Breizh, 112

L
La Baule-Escoublac, 13, 95
La Borderie, 8, 25, 26

La Brière, 93c
La Chalotais, 124
La Rouerie, marquis of, 121c
La Téne, culture of, 20c
La Tour, Jean Louis, 39c
Lac de Guerlédan, 12
Laita, 84
Lalaisse, 126
Lamballe, 9c, 132, 136c
Lampaul-Guimilau, 118, 118c
Lancelot, 8, 99, 100, 101c
Landevennec, abbey of, 26c
Langonnet, 111, 111c
Lann Gough, 106
Lannion, 12, 132
Lannion, bay of, 25, 44
Lanveaux, 102, 105, 109
Largoet, castle of, 105, 105c
Laz, 112c
Le Braz, Anatole, 35, 69, 78, 132
Le Bris, Miche, 73
Le Conquet, 12, 75c
Le Drezen, Christian, 126
Le Goff, Daniel, 112
Le Gonidec de Tressan, Count, 35
Le Grande, Alain, alias Barbetorte, 25c, 28, 95, 105
Le Mercier d'Erm, Camille, 56
Le Moyne de la Borderie, Arthur, 121c
Le Penven, Jeff, 86, 86c
Le Roux, Alain, 28c
Le Roux, Francois, 99
Le Roux, Louis-Napoleon, 36
Le Viol, Jean-Michel, 130c
Le Voyer, Dorig, 130c
Léchiagat, 82c
Léon, 12, 21, 40, 44c, 75, 118, 126
Les Abers, 12
Les Sept Îles Trégastel, 12
Lézardieux, 62
Lié, 12
Lignol, 111
Lir, 44
Litania, 99
Locmariaquer, 18, 88
Locminé, 12, 102
Locoal, 86
Locquirec, 73
Locronan, 132
Loctudy, 82c
Lollain, 8
Loonois, Tristan de, 8
Loquirec, 12
Lorient, 12, 37c, 84, 86, 86c, 106, 129
Louédin, Bernard, 56
Louppe, Albert, 44c
Louis the Pious, 26, 26c, 112
Louis XI, 30, 31c
Louis XII, 30
Louis XIV, 124
Louis XV, 124
Louis XVI, 32

M
Mael-Carhaix, 112
Mahè, 102
Mahé de la Bourdonnais, 53
Maine, 21
Malgorn, Theo, 77c
Malo, priest, 25
Mane Gwenn, 105
Manez Cam, manor of, 112
Mans, 21c, 35
Maodez, 60c, 62, 132
Marchese de la Rouerie, 32
Marie, Robert, 130c
Markale, Jean, 105
Marle, 91c
Martray, Joseph, 37
Masson, Erwan, 77, 75c
Maurice, Honoré, 112
Maximillian of Austria, 30
Méheut, Mathurin, 136c
Meiffret, Laurence
Mélar, 132
Mené, 114
Menec, 88, 88c
Menez Arre, 116
Menez Bré, 66, 132
Menez Hom, 114
Menez Kronan, 114c

Menez Meur, 116
Menez Mikael, 114, 114c
Merle, 9c
Merlin, 8, 18, 40, 99c, 100, 100c, 116
Merrien, 82
Meu, 13
Miliau, 132
Millardet, 124c
Minard, 60c
Molène, archipelago of, 70c
Molène, 12, 75, 75c, 77, 77c, 114c
Monet, Claude, 86c
Monfort, 93
Monjarret, Polig, 37, 37c, 130c
Monmouth, Geoffrey de, 99
Mont Saint Michel, 13, 46, 48c, 69
Monteneuf, 102
Montfort, Jean de, 28, 28c
Montmartre, 60
Montmuran, castle of, 121c
Morbihan, 22c, 102, 111, 111c
Morbihan, gulf of, 18c, 23, 88c, 91c
Morgan, 69, 100, 118
Morlaix, 12, 35
Morlaix, bay of, 12, 73, 73c
Morrigan, 40
Morvan, 26, 26c, 112
Motreff, 112
Mougau, 116
Musée Dobrée, 95
Muzillac, 102
Myrdhin, 130

N
Namneti, 21, 21c
Nancon, 121c
Nantes, 13, 21, 21c, 25c, 28, 31c, 37c, 86, 95, 95c, 97c, 124
Nantes, Canal de, 12
Napoleone, 32
Navarra, 95
Newgrange, 18
Nicolas le Grand, 112
Nogués, Kristenn, 130
Nominoé, 91, 103c
Nominoé-Nevenoe, 26
Nona, 132
Normandy, 13, 21, 46, 48c, 121
Normans, the, 95
Notre Dame du Roncier, basilica of, 109c

O
Obelix, 21, 88c
Oceanopolis, 44, 44c
Odet, 11, 12, 84c
Oisismes, 21, 116
Ouessant, 60c, 77c, 78, 80c, 81c, 116
Oust, 12, 102, 109, 109c

P
Paimpol, 12, 42, 44, 60, 60c, 62, 62c
Paimpont, forest of, 13, 109
Paon, 60
Paris, 12, 31c, 32, 33, 35, 35c, 126, 130
Patton, general, 53, 53c
Pays Bigouden, 11c
Pays Nantais, 93
Pearse, Padraig, 36
Pen Duick IV, 40
Penmarc'h, 40, 78
Penthièvre, 9c, 93
Penthièvre, Jeanne de, 28
Penvenan, 66, 69
Perrin, 126
Perros, Georges, 82
Perros-Guirec, 12, 66, 66c, 70, 70c, 129
Pichard, captain, 84
Picts, the, 25
Pierres Droites de Monteneuf, 102c
Pink Granite Coast, 66, 66c
Pléneuf Val André, 58c
Plessis Macé, edict of, 31c
Pleubian, 66
Pleumeur Bodou, 69
Plodaulmézeau, 39c
Ploermel, 109
Ploezal, 64c
Plogastel Saint Germain, church of, 21
Plomée fountain, 64c

Ploubazlanec, 60
Plouezoc'h, 73
Plougastel, 126
Plougrescant, 66
Ploumanach, 44, 66, 66c, 73c
Plourivo, 28
Plutarco, 46c
Poher, 26, 112
Pointe de Penmarch, 12
Pointe de Pern, 77c
Pointe de Poulains, 46c
Pointe de Saint Mathieu, 12
Pollaouenn, 126
Pont-Aven, 82, 129, 129c
Pont-l'Abbé, 128c, 129c
Pontcalleck, 32, 111
Pontivy, 12, 106, 106c
Porhoet, 102c, 109c
Pors Beac'h, 44
Port-Anna, 46c
Port-Coton, 86c
Portsall, 75
Portsmouth, 55c
Postumius, 99
Poul Fetan en Quistinic, 88c, 106, 106c
Primel, 73c
Primel-Tregastel, 73, 73c
Prussians, the, 35, 75

Q
Quelven, 106
Quénéquan, 106, 106c
Questembert, 105, 105c
Quiberon, 12, 18c, 23, 33
Quiberon, bay of, 12, 41c
Quimper, 12, 84, 84c, 126, 129, 129c, 130c
Quimperlé, 12, 84
Quistinic, 106, 106c
Qunipily, 105

R
Raffarin, 39
Raghenold, 25c
Rance, 13, 37c, 53, 53c, 56, 123
Rhedones, 13, 27c, 102, 102c, 103c
Redones, 21
Relecq, abbey of, 116
Renan, Ernest, 69, 69c, 132
Rennes, 8c, 11c, 13, 21, 21c, 28, 30, 35, 37c, 102c, 105, 106, 111, 123, 123c, 124, 124c
Renote, 73c
Rhuys, peninsula of, 88, 88c
Richemont-Richmond, county of, 28c
Rieux, 30, 105, 105c
Riguidel, 40
Rion, 60c
Roc'h Allaz, 66
Roc'h Trevézel, 114
Roche Jagut, 62, 64c
Rochefort en Terre, 102, 102c, 105
Rohan, 30, 106
Rohan, Marguerite de, 109c
Romans, the, 21c, 23, 26
Roparz, Loeiz, 126
Rosbras, 82
Roscoff, 12, 75, 75c
Roudouallec, 112
Rouerie, 121
Rouzic, island of, 70

S
Sable d'Or le Pins, 56c
Saint-Aubin du Cormier, 29c, 30
Saint Briac, 37c, 58c
Saint Brieuc, 12, 42c, 46
Saint Cornely, 88c
Saint-Denis, cathedral of, 31c
Saint Efflam, bay of, 66
Saint'Evre, Gillot, 31c
Saint Fiacre, chapel of, 111c
Saint Gildas, 105c
Saint Guénolé, 12, 25
Saint Guirec, oratory of, 66c
Saint-Jean du Doigt, 73c
Saint Juste, 102
Saint-Malo, 8c, 13, 37c, 40, 42, 53, 53c, 55c, 121, 123, 123c
Saint-Mathieu, abbey of, 75, 75c
Saint Maurice, chapel of, 58c
Saint Michel, chapel of, 56c

Saint-Nazaire, 13, 37c
Saint-Pierre, cathedral of, 95
Saint Pol Aurelien, 116
Saint Pol Roux, 11, 46, 46c
Saint Potan, 18c
Saint-Ronan, 132
Saint-Saveur, abbey of, 103c, 123
Saint Tanguy, 116
Saint Thégonnec, church of, 118, 118c
Saint-Tudwal, 69c
Saint-Tudwal, cathedral of, 69c
Saint Yves, 69c
Sainte Barbe, chapel of, 111c
Saint Ann, 46c
Sassenachs, 36
Saxons, the, 25, 25c
Scilly, 23
Scotland, 8
Sein, island of, 78, 78c
Sènes, 78c
Servat, Gilles, 86, 93c, 130
Seven Islands, archipelago of the, 66c, 70, 70c
Sienkievicz, 66
Solidor, tower of, 53
Solomon, King, 28
Sorligues, 23
Souvestre, Emile, 132
Spezet, 112
Squiban, Didier, 77
St-Germain-en Laye, 18c
Stivell, Alain, 39c, 86, 86c, 111, 130
Sulim, 105, 106
Surcouff, 8, 40, 53
Suscinio, castle of, 88, 88c

T
Tabarly, Eric, 40, 41c
Talbert, peninsula of, 66
Tanguy, 44c
Taureau, 73, 73c
Tir na n'Og, 118
Tolosa, 40
Tombelaine, island of, 46, 48c
Toullaeron, 112
Tréal, 102
Treburden, 66, 66c
Trécesson, castle of, 101c
Trécesson, Jean de, 100c
Trégastel, 21, 73c
Trégor, 12, 40, 62, 66, 75, 132
Treguier, 25c, 69, 69c
Trèpassè, bay of, 8, 46c, 78, 78c
Tri Yann, 130
Trieux, 12, 62, 64c
Triskell, 130
Tristam, 129
Troyes, Chrétien, de, 99
Tuchen Gador, 114
Tudual, 25, 132
Tuilerie, 35

U
Uxisama, 80c

V
Val Piriou, 126
Vannes, 9c, 12, 21, 31, 35c, 46c, 80c, 91, 91c, 105, 106, 106c, 124, 129c, 130c
Vannetais, 88c
Vauban, 55c, 86c
Vefa de Saint Pierre, countess of, 112, 112c
Vendome, 28
Veneto, natives of, 21, 21c, 22c, 23, 88, 88c, 91c
Verdun, 37c
Vieille, 78
Vikings, the, 25c
Vilaine, 13, 102, 121c
Vitré, 121, 121c
Viviane, 8, 40, 101c
Vorgium, 23, 112

W
Wace, Robert, 99
Wales, 8, 23, 75c
William the Conqueror, 28c
Wilson, Lambert, 56

Y
Yeun Elez, 114, 114c

PHOTO CREDITS

Livio Bourbon/Archivio White Star: pages 1, 8, 8-9, 9 top, 14-15, 42 top, 42 center, 42 bottom, 42-43, 43 top left, 43 top right, 44 bottom, 48 top, 48 bottom, 50 top left, 50 top right, 53 right center top, 53 right center bottom, 53 bottom right, 54 top left, 54 top right, 54-55, 55 top, 56 top, 56 bottom, 57 top left, 57 top right, 58 bottom, 59 top, 61 top, 62 top, 62-63, 63 top, 64 top, 64 center, 64 bottom, 64-65, 68 top left, 68 top right, 68-69, 69 left, 69 top right, 69 bottom right, 82 top, 82 bottom, 82-83, 83 top left, 84 top, 84 bottom, 84-85, 85 top left, 85 top right, 88 top, 90 top left, 90 top right, 90-91, 91 left, 91 top right, 91 bottom right, 93 top, 93 center, 93 bottom, 97 bottom right, 100 top, 100 center, 100 bottom, 101 top, 118 top, 118 bottom, 118-119, 119 top left, 119 top right, 120 top left, 120 top right, 120-121, 121 top, 121 center, 121 bottom, 122 top left, 122 top right, 122-123, 123 top, 124 top left, 124 bottom left, 124 top right, 124 center right, 124 bottom right, 125, 136.
Luciano Ramires/Archivio White Star: pages 50-51, 51 top, 51 bottom, 53 left, 78 bottom, 86 center.

136 On the corner of a building in the old quarter of Lamballe, a small town on the Cote D'Armor famous for its splendid stables that are open to the public, is the entrance to the little museum that was set up in honour of the local painter Mathurin Méheur (1882-1958).

David Ademas/Gamma/Contrasto: pages 39 top, 39 bottom.
Aisa: pages 26 bottom, 27, 30-31.
Bernard Annebique/Corbis Sygma/Grazia Neri: pages 80 top, 80-81, 81 top, 88-89, 127.
The Art Archive: pages 21 top, 26 top, 28.
J. G. J. G. Berizzi/RMN: pages 18 top.
Jean Arthus Bertrand/Corbis/Contrasto: pages 44-45, 58-59, 70-71, 72-73, 74 top right, 75 bottom, 95.
Bettmann/Corbis/Contrasto: pages 36-37.
Gérard Blot/RMN: page 18 bottom.
Yvon Boelle: pages 40 top, 40 bottom, 40-41, 41 top, 46 bottom, 46-47, 47 top right, 58 top, 60 top, 60 center, 60 bottom, 60-61, 62 bottom, 66 left, 70 top, 71 top left, 71 top right, 73 top, 73 center, 73 bottom, 74 top left, 76, 77 top, 77 bottom left, 77 bottom center, 77 bottom right, 78-79, 83 top right, 88 bottom, 89 top right, 98 top left, 98 top right, 98-99, 99 top, 100-101, 102 bottom, 103 top right, 105 top left, 105 top right, 106, 106-107, 107 top left, 107 top right, 109 top, 110 top left, 110-111, 112, 117 top, 130 left, 130 bottom right.
Christophe Boisvieux: pages 16-17, 102 top, 102-103, 103 top left, 104, 105 bottom, 108, 109 bottom, 110 top right, 111 top, 114 top, 114 bottom, 129 bottom.
Collezione privata: page 35.
The Bridgeman Art Library: pages 25, 28-29.
Henri Cartier-Bresson/Magnum/Contrasto: pages 38-39.
Jean Marc Charles/Corbis Sygma/Grazia Neri: pages 96-97.
Matthieu Colin/Hémisphères: pages 47 top left, 86 top, 86-87.
Giovanni Dagli Orti: pages 2/7, 22, 30 bottom, 31.
Leonard De Selva/Corbis/Contrasto: page 36 top right.
Jean-Yves Elaudais/Bodadeg ar Sonerion: page 38 bottom.
Gilles Guittar/Hoa-Qui: page 130 top left.
Chris Hellier/Corbis/Contrasto: pages 74-75.
John Elk III/Lonely Planet Images: page 89 top left.
Robert Estall/Corbis/Contrasto: page 123 bottom.
Fantuz/Sime: pages 92-93.
Didier Houeix: pages 10 top, 10-11, 11, 112-113.
Hervé Hughes/Hémisphères: pages 58 center, 62 center.
Hulton Archive/Grazia Neri: page 36 top left.
Hulton-Deutsch Collection/Corbis/Contrasto: pages 34-35.
M. Lanini/Panda Photo: page 116 top.
F. Latreille/Hoa Qui: page 45 top left.
J. P. Lescourret/Hémisphères: pages 66-67.
Erich Lessing/Contrsto: page 19.
S. Meyers/Panda Photo: page 116 bottom.
Musée des Beaux Arts de Quimper: page 32.
A. Petretti/Panda Photo: page 45 top right.
Jean-Charles and Christine Pinheira: pages 44 top, 97 bottom left, 126, 128 top left, 128 top right, 128-129, 129 top, 131.
Bertrand Rieger/Corbis Sygma/Grazia Neri: page 86 bottom.
Bertrand Rieger/Hémisphères: pages 46 top, 78 top, 79 top.
Guido Alberto Rossi: pages 48-49, 52, 53 top right, 87 top.
Sandford/Explorer/Hoa-Qui: pages 116-117.
Scala Archive: pages 23, 24.
M. Scataglini/Marka: pages 114-115.
Scope: pages 70 bottom, 111 bottom.
Setboun/Corbis/Contrasto: pages 94-95, 97 top right.
Giovanni Simeone/SIE: pages 3/6.
Giovanni Simeone/Sime: pages 56-57.
Lee Snider/Corbis/Contrasto: page 72 top.
Guy Thouvenin/Explorer/Hoa-Qui: page 75 top.
TopFoto/Icp: page 29 bottom.
Tony Vaccaro/Corbis Sygma/Grazia Neri: page 37 bottom.
E. Valentin/Hoa-Qui: page 97 top left.
Roger Viollet/Alinari: pages 32-33, 37 top.
Werner Forman Archive/Index: pages 20 left, 20 right, 21 bottom left, 21 bottom center, 21 bottom right.
Nick Wheeler/Corbis/Contrasto: page 80 bottom.
P. Wysocki/S. Frances/Hémisphères: pages 66 right, 67 top.
Patrick Zachmann/Magnum/Contrasto: pages 113 top left, 113 top right.
Bruno Zanzottera: pages 96 top, 132 top, 132 bottom, 133.